634
0005
634 Texaco
0985

3-8-81

Maclaren's Sermon Outlines

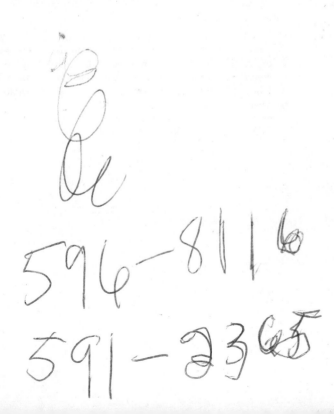

596-8116

591-2365

"It is difficult to believe that Dr. Maclaren's EXPOSITIONS will ever be superseded. Will there ever again be such a combination of spiritual insight, of scholarship, of passion, of style, of keen intellectual power? He was clearly a man of genius. So long as preachers care to teach from the Scriptures, they will find him their best guide and help. We shall not see his like again." — W. Robertson Nicoll, D.D., LL.D., Editor of *The Expositor's Bible* and *The Expositor's Greek Testament*, in *The British Weekly*.

"For 50 years he (Maclaren) continued as a Bible preacher, and in the midst of that period he began to be called the 'Prince of Expositors.' Perhaps, apart from Spurgeon and Moody, no man has had his sermons read by as many people as this great but plain preacher. Maclaren should be in every preacher's library. Read Maclaren to see expository preaching at its best." — Dr. Will H. Houghton, in *The Moody Monthly*, Jan., 1938.

"I have always found that my own comfort and efficiency in preaching have been in direct proportion to the frequency and depth of daily communion with God. I know of no way in which we can do our work but (1) quiet fellowship with Him; (2) resolute keeping up of a student's habits, which needs some power of saying 'no'; (3) conscientious pulpit preparation. The secret of success in everything is trust in God and hard work." — *Maclaren*.

The World's Great Sermons in Outline

Maclaren's
SERMON OUTLINES

A CHOICE COLLECTION OF THIRTY-FIVE MODEL SERMONS

by

ALEXANDER MACLAREN

THE "PRINCE OF PREACHERS"

Author of the Famous
EXPOSITIONS OF HOLY SCRIPTURE

Selected and Edited by

SHELDON B. QUINCER, D. D.
Baptist Theological Seminary
Grand Rapids, Michigan

WM. B. EERDMANS PUBLISHING COMPANY
Grand Rapids   Michigan

ISBN 0-8028-1156-6

Library of Congress Number 54-6232

FOREWORD

Alexander Maclaren was born in Glasgow, Scotland, and educated in England where he spent most of his long life. He served two churches, namely, Portland Chapel, Southampton, for ten years and Union Chapel, Manchester, for over a period of forty-five years.

Pre-eminently a preacher, Dr. Maclaren well deserves to be known as "the Prince of Bible Expositors." In recognition of his pulpit attainments the University of Edinburgh bestowed upon him the degree of Doctor of Divinity. His sermons are considered models in structure and content.

In addition to his *Expositions of Holy Scripture*,[1] for which he is best known, more than twenty other volumes of his sermons have been published, which are now out of print and difficult to obtain. In the compilation of this volume the editor has limited his selection of sermons from these lesser known and more or less hard to secure works.

The reader will recognize as he reads this volume that an effort has been made to include a wide variety of sermons both as to subjects and texts. The subject matter includes doctrinal, devotional, evangelistic, and biographical material. As to texts only a few times has more than one text been taken from one book of the Scriptures. An effort has been made to select texts from as many sections of the Bible as possible. There are texts from thirty-one books — thirteen from the Old Testament and eighteen from the New.

The purpose in preparing this volume for publication is not that the sermons may be preached verbatim, but to aid the young preacher or the layman who is untrained in the science of sermonizing and sometimes called upon to bring a Bible message, in the better preparation of his sermons or messages; thereby making him a more effective messenger of the Word of Truth. With this

---

1. Published in eleven volumes by the Wm. B. Eerdmans Publishing Co.

end in view the sermons have been outlined in more detail than usually found in the original volumes. They have also been abridged. That which has been considered the best of the content of the sermons has been retained to make the outlines intelligible and suggestive. It should also be stated that on the first page of each sermon outline the volume from which it was taken is indicated.

It is the earnest prayer of the editor that *Maclaren's Sermon Outlines* will be used to the glory of our Lord and Savior Jesus Christ and to the blessing of all who read and use them.

Sheldon B. Quincer

Grand Rapids, Michigan
March, 1954

CONTENTS

Maclaren's Sermon Outlines

1

Joseph's Faith

> *Joseph took an oath of the children of Is-*
> *rael, saying, God will surely visit you, and*
> *ye shall carry up my bones from thence.*
> —Genesis 50:25*

THIS is the one act of Joseph's life which the author of the Epistle to the Hebrews selects as the sign that he, too, lived by faith. "By faith Joseph, when he died, made mention of the departing of the children of Israel; and gave commandment concerning his bones" (Hebrews 11:22). It was at once a proof of how entirely he believed God's promise, and of how earnestly he longed for its fulfilment. It was a sign, too, of how little he felt himself at home in Egypt, though to outward appearance he had become completely one of its people.

I. FAITH IS ALWAYS THE SAME, THOUGH KNOWLEDGE VARIES.

A. **The Difference Between Creed and Faith.** The one may vary, does vary, within very wide limits; the other remains the same. The things believed have been growing from the beginning — the attitude of mind and will by which they have been grasped has been the same from the beginning and will be the same to the end. The contents of faith, that on which it relies, the treasure it grasps, changes; the essence of faith, the act of reliance, the grasp which holds the treasure, does not change.

1. *Creed varies.*

2. *Essence of faith never changes.*

---

* From *Sermons Preached in Manchester*, Third Series.

B. The Patriarchal Creed and Faith.

1. *Although the Patriarchal creed was imperfect, yet they had a clear knowledge of God.* They knew his inspiring, guiding presence; they knew the forgiveness of sins; they knew, though they very dimly understood, the promise, "In thy seed shall all the families of the earth be blessed" (Gen. 28:14).

2. *In Patriarchal times as well as now faith was necessary to salvation.* Joseph and his ancestors were joined to God by the very same bond which unites us to Him. There has never been but one path of life: "They *trusted* God and were lightened, and their faces were not ashamed."

C. The Relation of Creed to Faith.

1. *Creed does not save.* Brethren, what makes a Christian is not the theology you have in your heads, but the faith and love you have in your hearts.

2. *Creed is necessary to saving faith.* There can be no saving faith in an unseen Person except through the medium of thoughts concerning Him, which thoughts put into words are a creed. "Christ" is a mere name, empty of all significance till it be filled with definite statements of who and what Christ is.

II. FAITH HAS ITS NOBLEST OFFICE IN DETACHING FROM THE PRESENT.

A. Detachment From Worldly Surroundings. Joseph's dying words open a window into his soul and betray how little he had felt that he belonged to the order of things in the midst of which he had been content to live. We may be sure that, living, the hope of the inheritance must have burned in his heart as a hidden light and made him an alien everywhere but on its blessed soil.

1. *Joseph's detachment from worldly surroundings did not make him discontented with his earthly environment and responsibilities.*

2. *Joseph's detachment from worldly surroundings is revealed in his dying words.*

B. **Requirements For Detachment From Worldly
Surroundings.**

1. *Thoughts must be directed by faith in God.* If the unseen
is ever to rule in men's lives it must be through their
thoughts. It must become intelligible, clear, real. Such
certitude is given by faith alone.

2. *Desires must be directed by faith in God.* If the unseen is
ever to rule in men's lives it must become not only an object
to certain knowledge, but also for ardent wishes. It must
cease to be doubtful and must seem infinitely desirable.

C. **Benefits of Living a Life Detached From the World.**

1. *Discipline.* A man that is living for remote objects is, in
so far, a better man than one who is living for the present.
He will become thereby the subject of a mental and moral
discipline that will do him good.

2. *Change of character.* Whatever makes a man live in the
past and in the future raises him; but high above all others
stand those to whom the past is an apocalypse of God, with
Calvary for its center, and all the future is fellowship with
Christ, and joy in the heavens.

3. *Change of center of interest.* This change of the center of
interest from earth to heaven is the uniform effect of faith.
"Abraham," says the New Testament, "dwelt in tabernacles,
for he looked for a city" (Hebrews 11:8-10).

III. **FAITH MAKES MEN ENERGETIC IN THE
DUTIES OF THE PRESENT.**

A. **Joseph Was Faithful in His Duties in the World.**

1. *The world's sneer that Christianity makes a man indifferent
to activity in this present life.*

2. *Joseph's life contradicts the world's sneer.* Joseph was a
true Hebrew all his days. But that did not make him run
away from Pharaoh's service. He lived by hope and that

made him the better worker in the passing moment and kept him tugging away all his life at the oar, administering the affairs of a kingdom.

B. Duties of the Present Life Become Greater to the Persons Realizing the Reality of Heaven.

1. *The things of the present life are made less in their power to absorb or trouble.*

2. *The things of the present life are made greater in importance as preparations for what is beyond.*

C. Faith Energizes Man for Work.

1. *The reason*: Faith will energize us for any sort of work, seeing that it raises all to one level and brings all under one sanction and shows all as cooperating to one end.

2. *The illustration*: The muster-roll of the heroes of faith in the Epistle to the Hebrews (Ch. 11) marks the variety of grades of human life represented there, all fitted for their tasks and delivered from the snare that was in their calling by that faith which raised them above the world and therefore fitted them to come down on the world with stronger strokes of duty.

3. *The secret*: Trust Christ, live with Him and by hope of the inheritance.

CONCLUSION

Let us see that our clearer revelation bears fruit in a faith in the great Divine promises as calm and firm as this dying Patriarch had. Then the same power will work not only the same detachment and energy in life, but the same calmness and solemn light of hope in death.

2

Moses and Hobab

> *And Moses said unto Hobab . . . Leave us
> not, I pray thee; forasmuch as thou know-
> est how we are to encamp in the wilder-
> ness, and thou mayest be to us instead of
> eyes.* —Numbers 10:29, 31*

THE fugitives whom Moses led reached Sinai in three
months after leaving Egypt. They remained there for at least nine
months. Some time before the encampment broke up, a relative
of Moses by marriage, Hobab by name, had come into camp on
a visit. He was a Midianite by race, one of the wandering tribes
from the south-east of the Arabian Peninsula. He knew every
foot of the ground. So Moses, who had no doubt forgotten much
of the little desert skill he had learned in keeping Jethro's flock,
prays Hobab to remain with them and give them the benefit of
his practical knowledge.

I. A SENSE OF THE UNKNOWN WILDERNESS BEFORE US.

A. **A General Complexion of the Future May Be Roughly
Estimated.** We know very early in life that the thread of
our days is a mingled strand and the prevailing tone a sober,
neutral tint. The main characteristics of what we shall meet
we well enough know.

B. **The Particular Events of the Future Are Hidden.** It is
strange and impressive when we come to think how Providence, working with the same uniform materials in all human
lives, can yet, like some skilful artist, produce endless novelty
and surprises in each life. The solemn ignorance of the next

---

* From *The Secret of Power.*

15

moment is sometimes stimulating and joyous. But to all there
come times when their ignorance is saddening.

C. The Aspect of Life Represented as a Wilderness. There
are dangers and barren places and a great solitude in spite of
love and companionship, and many marchings and lurking
foes, and grim rocks, and fierce suns, and parched wells, and
shadeless sand wastes enough in every life to make us quail
often and look grave always when we think of what may be
before us.

II. AN ILLUSTRATION OF THE WEAKNESS THAT CLINGS TO HUMAN GUIDES.

A. The True Meaning of the Text. The true lesson of the
incident considered in connection with the following section is
that for men who have God to guide them it argues weakness
of this faith and courage to be much solicitous of any Hobab to
show them where to go and where to camp.

B. The True Meaning of the Text Does Not Exclude Human
Guides.

1. *Self-trained men are usually incomplete.* Fanciful notions
   take possession of the solitary thinker, and peculiarities of
   character that would have been kept in check, and might
   have become aids in the symmetrical development of the
   whole man, if they had been reduced and modified in
   society, get swollen into deformities in solitude.

2. *Much of God's guidance is through men.* God's guidance
   does not make man's needless, for a very large part of God's
   guidance is ministered to us through men. And wherever
   a man's thoughts and words teach us to understand God's
   thoughts and words more clearly, to love them more earnestly, or to obey them more gladly, there human guidance
   is discharging its noblest function.

C. The Danger to be Avoided. We are ever apt to feel that we
cannot do without the human leader. Our weakness of faith
in the unseen is ever tending to pervert the relation between

teacher and taught into practical forgetfulness that the promise of the new covenant is, "They shall be all taught of God" (John 6:45).

1. *Avoid overemphasizing human guidance.*

2. *Avoid underestimating Divine guidance.*

III. THE TRUE LEADER OF OUR MARCH.

A. **Israel's True Leader.** The true leader of the children of Israel in their wilderness journey was not Moses, but the Divine Presence in the cloud with a heart of fire, that hovered over their camp for a defense and sailed before them for a guide. Exodus 13:21

B. **The Christian's True Leader.** In sober reality we have God's presence; and waiting hearts which have ceased from self-will may receive leading as real as ever the pillar gave to Israel.

C. **The Christian's Responsibility to His Leader.**

1. *Obedient step by step following.* No doubt in all our lives there come times when we seem to have been brought into a blind alley, and cannot see where we are to get out; but it is very rare indeed that we do not see one step in advance, the duty which lies next to us. And be sure of this, that if we are content to see but one step at a time, and take it, we shall find our way made plain.

2. *Certainty of God's will.* Do not seek to outrun God's guidance, to see what you are to do a year hence or to act before you are sure of what is His will; do not let your wishes get in advance of the pillar and the ark, and you will be kept from many a mistake and led into a region of deep peace.

3. *Reverent following.* "Go after the ark, yet there shall be a space between it and you; come not near it, that ye may know the way ye ought to go" (Joshua 3:3, 4). If we impatiently press too close on the heels of our guide we loose the guidance. There must be a reverent following

which allows indications of the way full time to develop themselves and does not fling itself into new circumstances on the first flush of apparent duty.

IV. THE CRAVING FOR A HUMAN GUIDE HAS BEEN MET IN THE GIFT OF CHRIST.

A. **Hobab's Qualification.** Moses sought to secure this Midianite guide because he was a native of the desert and had travelled all over it. His experience was his qualification.

B. **Christ's Qualification.** He travelled every foot of the road by which we have to go. He knows "how to encamp in this wilderness," for He himself has "tabernacled among us" and by experience has learned the weariness of the journey and the perils of the wilderness.

C. **The Believer's Pattern.** His life is our pattern. Our marching orders are brief and simple: Follow your leader, and plant your feet in His footprints.

CONCLUSION

If we only ask Him to be with us "instead of eyes" and accept His gentle leading, we shall not walk in darkness, but may plunge into thickest night and the most unknown land, assured that He will "lead us by the right way to the city of habitation" (Psalm 107:7).

3

The Eagle and Its Brood

As an eagle stirreth up her nest, fluttereth over her young, spreadeth abroad her wings, taketh them, beareth them on her wings.   —Deuteronomy 32:11*

THIS is an incomplete sentence in the Authorized Version, but really it should be rendered as a complete one, the description of the eagle's action including only the two first clauses, and (the figure being still retained) the person spoken of in the last clauses being God Himself. That is to say, it should read thus, "As an eagle stirreth up his nest, fluttereth over his young, He spreads abroad His wings, takes them, bears them on His pinions." While the text primarily refers to the infant nation in the forty years wanderings, it carries larger truths about us all; and sets forth the true meaning and importance of life.

I. A GRAND THOUGHT ABOUT GOD.

A. The Metaphor Used: The Vulture. Now it may come as something of a shock if I say that the bird that is selected for the comparison is not really an eagle, but one which, in our estimation, is of a very much lower order — viz., the carnivorous vulture. Our modern repugnance to the vulture as feeding on carcases was probably not felt by the singer of this song. What he brings into view are the characteristics common to the eagle and the vulture; superb strength in beak and claw, keeness of vision almost incredible, magnificent sweep of pinion and power of rapid, unwearied flight.

B. The Purpose of the Use of the Metaphor: to show the analogy between the characteristics of the bird and the Divine

---

* From *Triumphant Certainties.*

nature. And these characteristics, we may say, have their analogies in the Divine nature, and the emblem not unfitly shadows forth one aspect of the God of Israel, who is "fearful in praises," who is strong to destroy as well as to save, whose all-seeing eye marks every foul thing, and who often pounces on it swiftly to rend it to pieces, though the sky seemed empty a moment before.

C. The Lesson Taught by the Metaphor. But the action described in the text is not destructive, terrible, or fierce. The monarch of the sky busies itself with tender cares, for its brood. Then, there is gentleness along with the terribleness. The impression of this blending of power and gentleness is greatly deepened, as it seems to me, if we notice that it is the male bird that is spoken about in the text, which should be rendered: "As the eagle stirreth up *his* nest and fluttereth over *his* young."

II. AN ILLUMINATING THOUGHT OF THE MEANING OF LIFE.

A. The Purpose of Life: a training school fitting the child of God for heaven. What is it all for? To teach us to fly, to exercise our half-fledged wings in the short flights, that may prepare us for, and make it possible to take, longer ones. Every event that befalls us has a meaning beyond itself; and every task that we have to do reacts upon us, the doers, and either fits or hinders us for larger work. Life as a whole, and in its minutest detail, is worthy of God to give, and worthy of us to possess, only if we recognize the teaching that is put into the picturesque form in this text — that the meaning of all which God does to us is to train us for something greater beyond.

B. The Importance of the Purpose of Life: it is the key to the mystery of life. No man gets to the heart of the mystery of life or has in his hand the key which will enable him to unlock all the doors and difficulties of human experience, unless he gets to this — that it is meant as training.

C. The Necessity to Carry Out This Conviction of the Purpose of Life in the Small Things. If we could only carry that clear conviction with us day by day into the little things of life, what different things these, which we call the monotonous trifles of our daily duties, would become. The things may be small and unimportant, but the way we do them is not unimportant. The same fidelity may be exercised and must be brought to bear in order to do the veriest trifle of our daily lives rightly, that needs to be invoked, in order to get us safely through the crises and great times of life.

III. A CALMING THOUGHT AS TO THE VARIETY OF GOD'S METHODS WITH US.

A. God's Loving Compulsion to Effort: "As the eagle stirreth up his nest."

1. *To "stir up the nest" means* to make a man uncomfortable where he is.

2. *The methods of stirring up the nest are varied* — sometimes by the prickings of man's conscience, sometimes by changes of circumstances, and oftentimes by sorrows.

3. *The reason for stirring up the nest.* We all shrink from change. What would we do if we had it not? We should stiffen into habits that would dwarf and weaken us. We all recoil from storms. What should we do if we had them not? Sea and air would stagnate, and would become heavy and putrid and pestilential, if it was not for the wild west wind and the hurtling storms. So all our changes and all our sorrows should be recognized as being what they are, loving summonses to effort.

B. God's Hovering Presence: "fluttereth over his young." It is a very beautiful word that is employed here which "flutter" scarcely gives us. It is the same that is used in the first chapter of Genesis, about the Spirit of God "brooding on the face of the waters"; and it suggests how near, how all protecting, with expanded wings the Divine Father comes to the child whose restfulness He has disturbed.

C. God's Sustaining Power: "He spreadeth abroad His wings; He taketh them; beareth them on His wings." On those broad pinions we are lifted and by them we are guarded. It is a picturesque way of saying, "Thou canst do all things through Christ which strengtheneth thee." The Psalmist sang that angels' hands should bear up God's servant. That is little compared with this promise of being carried heaven-wards on Jehovah's own pinions.

CONCLUSION

During life this training will go on; and after life, what then? Then, in the deepest sense, the old word will be true, "Ye know how I bore you on eagle's wings and brought you to myself"; and the great promise shall be fulfilled, when the half-fledged young brood are matured and full grown, "They shall mount up with wings as eagles; they shall not be weary; they shall walk and not faint."

4 *[handwritten: See p 27]*

Unpossessed Possessions

> *And the King of Israel said unto his serv-*
> *ants, Know ye that Ramoth in Gilead is*
> *ours, and we be still, and take it not out*
> *of the hand of the King of Syria?*
> —I Kings 22:3*

THIS city of Ramoth in Gilead was an important
fortified place on the eastern side of the Jordan and had been
captured by the northern neighbors in the kingdom of Syria. The
people of Israel backed up by a powerful alliance with Jehoshaphat
of Judah determined to make a dash to get back what was theirs.

I. WHAT IS OURS AND NOT OURS.

Every Christian ~~man~~ has large tracts of unannexed territory,
unattained possibilities, unenjoyed blessings, things that are
[handwritten: theirs] ~~his~~ and yet not ~~his~~ *[handwritten: theirs]*

A. Some Unpossessed Possessions.

1. *Undisturbed peace.* There may be a peace in our hearts
   deep as life; a tranquillity which may be superficially disturbed, but is never thoroughly, ~~and down~~ to the depths
   broken. ~~The peace of God is ours; but ah—in how sad a
   sense it is true~~ that the peace of God is *not* ours. *[handwritten: all the time]*

2. *Absolute Surrender.* It is well within the reach of every
   Christian soul that he or she should live day by day in the
   continual and utter surrender of himself or herself to the
   will of God. But instead of this absolute submission of
   ourselves to Him, what do we find?

---

* From *Christ's Musts.*

23

3. *Fulness of power.* The Divine gift to the Christian community and to the individuals who compose it is of fulness of power for all their work. And yet look how all through the ages the church has been beaten by the corruption of the world. *There is a Church of Darkness —* "

C. ~~The~~ Three-fold Title and Charter to Our Possessions.

1. *God's purpose.* God's purpose, which is nothing less for every one of us than that we should be "filled with all the fulness of God" (Ephesians 3:19), and that He should supply all our need "according to His riches in glory" (Philippians 4:19) — that is the first of the parchments on which our title depends.

2. *Christ's purchase.* And the second title-deed is Christ's purchase; for the efficacy of His death and the power of His triumphant life have secured for all that trust Him the whole fulness of this Divine Gift.

3. *Holy Spirit's influence.* And the third of our claims and titles is the influence of the Holy Spirit that Jesus Christ gives to every one of His children to dwell in Him. There is working in you, if you have any faith ~~in that~~ in Lord, a power that is capable of making you perfectly pure, perfectly blessed, strong with an immortal strength, and glad with a "joy unspeakable and full of glory."

II. ~~OUR~~ *There is a* STRANGE CONTENTMENT IN IMPERFECT POSSESSION.

A. The Reasons for This Strange Contentment. Ahab's remonstrances with his servants seem to suggest that there were two reasons for their acquiesence in the domination of a foreign power on ~~a bit of~~ their soil. They had not realized that Ramoth was theirs and they were too lazy and cowardly to go and take it.

1. *Ignorance of unattained possibilities in the Christian life.* That unfamiliarity with the thought of unattained possibilities in the Christian life is a curse of thousands of people who call themselves Christians. They do not think,

they never realize that it is possible for them to be ~~all~~ unlike what they are now.

2. *Love of ease.* Another reason for the woeful disproportion between what we have and what we utilize is the love of ease, such as kept these Israelites from going up to Ramoth-Gilead. On the whole it was more comfortable to sit at home or look after their farms and their merchandise than to embark on the unromantic attempt to win back a city that had not been theirs for ~~ever so~~ long and that they had got on very well without. *it is their possession*

B. The Seriousness of This Strange Contentment. ~~And is not~~ that *is* something like despising the birthright? Is it not a criminal thing for Christian people thus to neglect and put aside and never seek to obtain all these great gifts of God? There they lie at our doors and they are ours for the taking.

   1. *Is it not like despising our birthright?*

   2. *Is it not a criminal thing?* (*peace, joy, love popinessek,*

there is an
III. ~~THE~~ EFFORT THAT IS NEEDED TO MAKE OUR OWN OURS.

A. The Christian Must Take His Possessions. "We be still, and take it not out of the hands of the King of Syria." Then these things that are ours, by God's gift, by Christ's purchase, by the Spirit's influence will need our effort to secure them. And that is no contradiction nor any paradox. God does exactly in the same way with regard to His spiritual ones. He gives them to us, but we hold them on this tenure, that we put forth our best efforts to get and to keep them. His giving them does not set aside our taking. *we make one step etc*

   1. *They are God's gifts.*

   2. *They are to be taken by the Christian.*

there is a
B. The Necessity of Familiarizing Ourselves With the Possibilities of Unattained Possessions.

   1. *This applies to all spheres of life.* One large part of the discipline by which men make their own their own is by

familiarizing themselves with the thought of the larger possibilities of unattained possessions which God has given them. That is true in everything. To recognize our present imperfection and to see stretching before us glorious and immense possibilities is the salt of life in every region.

2. *Failure in this results in failure in growth.* Whosoever has once lost, or found becoming dim, the vision before him of a possible better than his present best, in any region, is in that region condemned to grow no more. If we desire to have any kind of advancement it is only possible for us when there gleams before us the untravelled road, and we see at the end of it unattained brightnesses and blessings.

CONCLUSION

Let us put away from ourselves this slothful indifference to our unattained possessions. "Know ye that Ramoth is ours?" "Let us be still no longer." "All things are yours, whether the world, or life, or death, or things present, or things to come: all are yours if ye are Christ's." *Some[?] us are so preoccupied in things material we fail to obtain things spiritually dont Be Complacent move on to higher better things (Church, job, Home)*

Satan is styled as a thief he steals all
God gives us life (God) death (satan) god-God
goodness (satan) etc

5

Pride Overcoming Want

> *But Naaman was wroth, and went away,
> and said, Behold, I thought he will surely
> come out to me, and stand, and call on the
> name of the Lord his God, and strike his
> hand over the place, and recover the leper.*
> —II Kings 5:11*

WITH soldier-like quickness of temper and pride, he flashes all at once into a blaze. Leper as he is, and having come there to beg a cure, he cannot stand this with patience; and in his wrath he lets us see curiously and naturally enough all his expectations, and what he thinks his reasonable ground of anger. The characteristics which offended Naaman are the characteristics of God's cure for the leprosy of our spirits.

I. THE UTTER INDIFFERENCE OF THE GOSPEL TO ALL DISTINCTIONS AMONG MEN.

A. The Fact That the Gospel Deals With All Men on the Same Level.

1. *The fact illustrated in Naaman's experience.* Naaman wanted to be treated as a great man that happened to be a leper: Elisha treated him as a leper that happened to be a great man. He did so not out of rudeness or caprice, but to bring this thought home to him: Your adventitious distinctions are of very small consequence as long as your skin shines with the ghastly whiteness of death.

2. *The fact stated.* The Gospel deals with all men as on one level. The community in the sickness of sin destroys all distinctions.

---

* From *Sermons Preached in Manchester*, Third Series.

B. The Reasons for the Gospel's Dealing With All Men on the Same Level.

1. *All men are sinners.* "All the world is guilty before God!" You cannot refute and you will not mend that old saying about man's condition. No other theory is so profoundly and accurately true, as that on which the Bible proceeds — the universal fact of sin, the universal guilt of sin, the universal burden of sin.

2. *Christ died for all men.* "He hath shut up all in unbelief that He might have mercy upon all" (Romans 11:32). As sin and death, so God's love and Christ's work know nothing of our superficial distinctions.

C. The Glory of the Gospel's Dealing With All Men on the Same Level. The superb indifference of the Gospel to all the distinctions of man from man, is its true glory and has wrought wonderful things.

1. *The glory of the Gospel is seen in that it, without respect of persons, delivers from sin's bondage.* The Gospel. the true democracy, came and struck the bonds from the slave.

2. *The glory of the Gospel is also seen in that it, without respect of persons, unifies believers.* We being many are one bread, "for we are all partakers of that one bread" (I Corinthians 10:17).

II. THE NAKED SIMPLICITY OF GOD'S GOSPEL.

A. Man's Way.

1. *The tendency of men portrayed in Naaman.* "Behold, I thought he will come and stand and call on the name of the Lord his God, and strike his hand over the place, and so by all that ceremonial he will recover the leper."

2. *The tendency of man is to look for some tangible object for his wavering confidences to lay hold upon.*

B. God's Method.

1. *God's method with Naaman.* It was like God to contradict the desire and to give him instead — only a promise to grasp and a command to obey.

2. *God's method in the Gospel.* The one power that cleanses is His blood for pardon, His Spirit for holiness. The one condition of receiving these is simple faith in Him; all externals are nothing.

C. Dangers to be Avoided.

1. *Sacramentalism.* The sense-bound materialism which sways us all lays hold of the pure Gospel which Christ wrought and gives and deforms it by tacking on to it an incongruous and heterogeneous appendage of rites and ceremonies and by investing the simple ordinances which He enjoined with mysterious power.

2. *The formalism of the non-conformist.* We are tempted to attach a false kind of value to church membership and to outward participation in Christian ordinances. We are constantly tempted to put the form in the place of the spirit.

III. THE UTTER REJECTION BY THE GOSPEL OF ALL MAN'S COOPERATION IN HIS OWN CLEANSING.

A. A Reason for Naaman's Rejection of the Requirement for Cleansing. The words of Naaman himself do not explicitly contain his refusal to do what was required, on the ground it was so small a thing. But that was evidently in his mind, as well as the other grounds of offence; and it comes out distinctly in the common-sense remonstrance by which his servants brought their angry master to reason — "If the prophet had bid thee do some great thing, wouldest thou not have done it? How much rather then, when he saith to thee, Wash and be clean" (II Kings 5:13).

B. **The Gospel Rejects Man's Cooperation in Salvation.** The characteristic of the Gospel is that it will have none of our work. Salvation, though not secured without our faith, cannot be said to be procured by our cooperation.

C. **The Gospel Rejects Man's Cooperation in Salvation Because the Gospel Demands Faith.**

1. *What faith is.* An essential part of faith is the consciousness that we can do nothing, the forsaking and going out of ourselves, accompanying the flight to Him. The under side of faith is self-abnegation; the upper side is confidence in Christ. Therefore, the proclamation that we are justified by faith is at the same time the absolute refusal to give men any share in their own healing.

2. *What faith does.* Faith is not the means of our cure, but only the bringing of our sickness into contact with the means. God's love in Christ, Christ's Spirit poured out — these are the energies that heal; faith is but lifting the eyelids that the light may fill the eyes, but opening the door that the physician may enter.

CONCLUSION

It is the glory of the Gospel that it proclaims a work in which we have no share. Christ will do it all. Nay, Christ has done it all. "Not by works of righteousness, but according to His mercy He saved us" (Titus 3:5).

Prudence and Faith

> And Amaziah said to the man of God, But
> what shall we do for the hundred talents
> which I have given to the army of Israel?
> And the man of God answered, The Lord
> is able to give thee much more than this.
> —II Chronicles 25:9*

WHEN Amaziah came to the throne he immediately
began to aim at conquests. In order to strengthen himself he hired
"a hundred thousand mighty men of valor" out of Israel for a
hundred talents of silver. To seek help from Israel was in the
prophet's eyes equivalent to flinging off help from God. So a
man of God comes to him and warns him that the Lord is not
with Israel and that the alliance is not permissible for him. Instead of yielding to the prophet's advice, Amaziah parries it with
this misplaced question.

I. A MISPLACED QUESTION.

A. The Reason This Was a Misplaced Question. I call it
misplaced because Amaziah's fault, and the fault of a great
many of us, was, not that he took consequences into account,
but that he took them into account at the wrong time. The
question should have come second, not first. Amaziah's first
business should have been to see clearly what was duty; and
then, the next business should have been to consider consequences.

1. *It was not a misplaced question because it took account of
consequences.*

---

* From *Last Sheaves*.

2. *It was a misplaced question because it took account of consequences at the wrong time.*

B. The Right Place and Way of Asking This Question.

1. *The tragedy of the failure to consider consequences.* Many of us make shipwreck of our lives because, with our eyes shut, we determine upon some grand design and fall under the condemnation of the man that "began to build and was not able to finish." If a man does not open his eyes to a clear vision of the consequences of his actions his life will go to water in all directions.

2. *The wisdom of considering consequences in the Christian life.* There is no region in which such clear insight into what is going to follow upon my determinations and the part that I take, is more necessary than in the Christian life. Let us face the facts of what is involved in the way of sacrifice, surrender, loss, if we determine to be on Christ's side; and then, when the difficulties come we shall neither be perplexed nor swept away.

C. The Right Thing in the Wrong Place.

1. *In the life of the individual.* Amaziah thought nothing about duty. There sprang up in his mind the cowardly and ignoble thought, "I cannot afford to do what is right because it will cost me a hundred talents." He that allows the clearest perception of disagreeable consequences to frighten him out of the road that he knows he ought to take is a fool, a coward and recreant to his own conscience.

2. *In the life of the church.* All the churches are too apt to let their eyes wander from reading the plain precepts of the New Testament to looking for the damaging results to be expected from keeping them.

3. *In the life of the nation.* The nation takes a leaf out of Amaziah's book and puts aside many plain duties for no better reason than that it would cost too much to do them. "What is the use of talking about suppressing the liquor

traffic. Think of the cost." The hundred talents block the way and bribe the national conscience.

II. THE TRIUMPHANT ANSWER.

A. The Meaning of the Prophet.

1. *The ability of God to give.* I suppose this prophet did not mean more than the undeniable truth that God was able to give Amaziah more than a hundred talents.

2. *The probability of God's giving.* He simply meant, "You will very likely get more than the one hundred talents that you have lost, if you do what pleases God."

B. The Wrong Application of the Prophet's Answer.

1. *In the Old Testament material prosperity did not always follow righteousness.* In the Old Testament we have instances enough that prosperity did not always attend righteousness. In the Old Testament we find the book of Job and the book of Ecclesiastes and many a Psalm, all of which were written in order to grapple with the question, "How is it that God does *not* give the good man more than the hundred talents he has lost for the sake of being good?"

2. *Today material prosperity does not always follow righteousness.* It is not true, and it is a dreadful mistake to suggest that it is true that a man in this world never loses by being a good, honest, consistent Christian. He often does lose a great deal as far as this world is concerned; and he has to make up his mind to lose it.

C. The Right Application of the Prophet's Answer.

1. *The gaining of nobility and strength of character.* The "much more" that Christianity has educated us to understand is meant in the depths of such a promise as this is, first of all, character. Every man that sacrifices anything to convictions of duty gains more than he loses thereby, because he gains in inward nobleness and strength, to say nothing of the genial warmth of an approving conscience.

2. *The gaining of a fuller capacity for a fuller possession of Christ.* He wins not only character, but a fuller capacity for a fuller possession of Jesus Christ Himself and that is infinitely more than anything that any man has ever sacrificed for the sake of that dear Lord. Do you remember when it was that there was granted to the Apostle John the vision of the enthroned Christ? It was "when I was in Patmos for the Word of God, and for the testimony of Jesus." He lost Ephesus; he gained an open heaven and a visible Christ.

CONCLUSION

Fling out the ballast if you wish the balloon to rise. Let the hundred talents go if you wish to get the "more than this." And listen to the New Testament variation of this Old Testament promise, "If thou wilt have treasure in heaven, go and sell all that thou hast and follow Me."

7

A Pattern Prayer

> *Bow down Thine ear, O Lord, hear me;
> for I am poor and needy. Preserve my
> soul; for I am holy: O Thou my God,
> save Thy servant that trusteth in Thee.
> Be merciful unto me, O Lord: for I cry
> unto Thee daily. Rejoice the soul of Thy
> servant: for unto Thee, O Lord, do I lift
> up my soul. For Thou, Lord, art good,
> and ready to forgive; and plenteous in
> mercy unto all them that call upon Thee.*
> **—Psalm 86:1-5***

W HEN ye pray, use not vain repititions, as the heathen
do." But earnest reiteration is not vain repitition. The one is
born of doubt; the other of faith. This faithful and prevailing
reiteration remarkably characterizes the striking series of supplica-
tions in these verses.

I. THE INVOCATIONS.

A. **The General Idea of Invocation.** When we call upon the
name of God aright we do three things:

1. *Contemplate the character of God.* We summon up before
   our thoughts that aspect of the Divine character which lies
   in the name that we utter.

2. *Profess to trust in that character of God revealed in the
   name.* We say in effect: "This aspect of Thy Divine all
   sufficiency, this fragment of thine ineffable perfection, on
   this I build and to this I make my appeal."

3. *Profess to believe that God responds to the obligations that
   are involved therein.* It is as saying: "I bring Thee myself

---

* From *Sermons Preached in Manchester*, Third Series.

and in Thy mighty name, for the sake of what it declares, I ask that these goods may be bestowed upon me."

B. The Comprehensiveness and Variety of God's Names Used by the Psalmist.

1. *Jehovah.* This name has a double force in Scripture — one derived from its literal, philological meaning; the other derived from its historical use and development. As concerns the former the word substantially implies eternal, timeless beings, underived self-existence. As to the latter, it was given as a seal of the covenant, as the ground of the great deliverance from Egyptian bondage.

2. *My God.* The word "God" implies the abundance and fulness of power. This general conception becomes special on the Psalmist's lips by the personal pronoun "my" which he prefixes to the name.

3. *Lord.* The name "Lord" is not the same word as that which is rendered *LORD* in verse 1. That, as we have said, is Jehovah. This means just what our English word "lord" means; it conveys the general idea of authority and dominion.

II. THE PETITIONS.

A. The Basis of Petitions: The Cry that God Will Hear.

1. *An act of the will is included in the hearing of prayer.* There is an act of loving will which is most clearly conveyed by that strong, and yet plain and intelligible metaphor, "Bow down thine ear," as an eager listener puts his hand to his ear and bends the lobe of it in the direction of the sound.

2. *Hearing embodied in an act of deliverance.* With God to hear is to answer.

B. A Description of the Process of Deliverance and the Need and Weakness of the Suppliant: the petition for protection, safety, and mercy.

1. *The deliverance contemplated.* The first petition, "preserve my soul," might be rendered, "guard" or "watch" my soul. Looking at all three we see that the first prays for protection; the second prays for the happy issue of that protection in safety; and the third prays for that mercy which is the sole foundation of both the protection and the safety it ensures.

2. *The suppliant's need and weakness revealed.* These three petitions also embody varying thoughts of the need and weakness of the suppliant. In the two former (vs. 2) he regards himself as defenseless and in peril. In the last (vs. 3) he thinks of himself as lowly and unworthy — for "mercy" is love shown to inferiors or to those who deserve something else.

3. *A significant omission.* In all this variety of petitions for deliverance there is not a word about the exact manner of it. The way in which God's mercy is to guard and save is left, with meek patience, to God's decision.

C. **The Petition for Gladness:** rejoice the soul of Thy servant.

1. *All of God's obedient children have a claim on God for joy.* All His creatures have a claim on Him for blessedness according to their capacity, as long as they stand where He has set them.

2. *God's disobedient children may have joy in returning to Him.* The persons who have departed from that obedience which is joy, may yet, in penitent abasement, return to Him and ask that He would rejoice the soul of His servant, Psalm 51:8.

III. **THE PLEAS.**

A. **The Psalmist Pleads His Necessities.** He is "poor and needy," or rather, perhaps, "afflicted and poor," borne down by the pressure of outward calamity and destitute of inward resources. Circumstances and character both constitute an appeal to God.

1. *Circumstances:* the evils that oppress from without.

2. *Character*: the lack of power within to bear up against outward circumstances.

B. The Psalmist Pleads His Relation to God and His Longing for Communion With God.

1. *His relationship expressed.* (a) "I am holy." The word in the original means "one who is the recipient or object of mercy." "One whom Thou favorest." It sets forth the relation between God and His suppliant from the divine side. (b) "Thy servant that trusteth in Thee." This is the same relation contemplated from the human side. I am knit to Thee, as a servant I belong to Thy household, and the Master's honor is concerned in His dependent's safety.

2. *His longing for fellowship expressed.* "Unto Thee do I lift up my soul." This expresses the conscious effort to raise his whole being above earth, to lift the heavy grossness of his nature bound in the fetters of sense to this low world, up and up to the Most High who is his home.

C. The Psalmist Pleads God's Own Character.

1. *This is the forceful plea with God.* The one prevalent plea with God is the faithful recounting of all that grace and pity which He is and has exercised.

2. *God is the reason and source of all our deliverance.* Because we can pray by none other, we implore Him by Himself, for the sake of His own holy Name, because He is that He is, to have mercy upon us.

CONCLUSION

When we call upon the name of Jesus Christ our Lord and ask that our prayers be heard "for the sake of Christ," we are taking no other plea into our lips than that ancient and all prevalent one of this Psalm.

8

From the Depths to the Heights

> *Out of the depths have I cried unto Thee
> O Lord. Lord hear my voice; let Thine
> ears be attentive to the voice of my suppli-
> cations. If Thou, Lord, shouldest mark
> iniquities, O Lord! who shall stand? But
> there is forgiveness with Thee, that Thou
> mayest be feared. I wait for the Lord, my
> soul doth wait, and in His word do I hope.
> My soul waiteth for the Lord more than
> they that watch for the morning: I say,
> more than they that watch for the morn-
> ing. Let Israel hope in the Lord; for with
> the Lord there is mercy, and with Him is
> plenteous redemption. And He shall re-
> deem Israel from all his iniquities.*
>
> —Psalm 130*

IT is a "song of degrees," as the heading tells us, that is, a "song of goings up." Whatever that very enigmatical phrase may mean, there is a sense in which this Psalm, at any rate, is distinctly a song of ascent, in that it starts from the very lowest point of self-abasement and consciousness of evil and rises steadily up to the tranquil summit, led by the consciousness of the Divine Presence and grace.

I. THE CRY FROM THE DEPTHS. Vss. 1-2.

A. The Meaning of "the Depths."

1. *It is not merely the depth of the recognition of man's insignificance, sorrow, or despondency.*

2. *It is primarily the depth of the recognition of man's sinfulness.*

---

* From *A Year's Ministry*, Second Series.

B. The Truths Suggested by the Cry from the Depths.

1. *The depths are the place for us all.* Every man amongst us has to go down there, if we take the place that belongs to us.

2. *Unless a man has cried to God from the depths he has never cried to Him at all.* Unless you come to Him as a penitent, sinful man, with the consciousness of transgression awakened within you, your prayers are shallow.

3. *Nothing more than a cry is needed to draw a man from the depths.* God has let down the fulness of His forgiving love in Jesus Christ our Lord, and all that we need is the call, which is likewise faith, which accepts while it desires, and desires in its acceptance; and then we are lifted up "out of an horrible pit and the miry clay," and our feet are set upon a rock, and our goings established. (Psalm 40:2.)

II. A DARK FEAR AND A BRIGHT ASSURANCE.
Vss. 3-4.

A. The Fear That God Will Mark Iniquities.

1. *To "mark iniquities" means to impute them to us.* The word, in the original, means to *watch,* that is to say, to remember in order to punish.

2. *The impossibility of any man sustaining the righteous judgment of God.* Like a man having to yield ground to an eager enemy, or to bend before the blast, every man has to bow before that flashing brightness and to own that retribution would be destruction.

B. The Assurance of Forgiveness.

1. *The significance of the term "forgiveness."* "Forgiveness!" The word so translated here in my text has for its literal meaning, "cutting off," "excision."

2. *The area of forgiveness.* Men may say, "There cannot be forgiveness; you cannot alter consequences." But forgiveness has not to do only with consequences; but also and

chiefly with the personal relation between me and God, and that can be altered.

3. *The basis of godliness is forgiveness.* No man reverences and loves and draws near to God so rapturously, so humbly, as the man that has learned pardon through Jesus Christ. "There is forgiveness with Thee, that Thou mayest be feared" (vs. 4).

III. DEPENDENCE UPON GOD. Vss. 5-6.

A. Its Nature.

1. *It is a permanent dependence.* A continual dependence upon God.

2. *It is a peaceful dependence.* They that have tasted that the Lord is gracius can sit very quietly at His feet and trust themselves to His kindly dealings, resting their souls upon His strong word, and looking for the fuller communication of light from Himself. This is a beautiful picture of a tranquil, continuous, ever-rewarded, and ever fresh waiting upon Him and reliance upon His mercy.

B. The Desire of the Man Depending Upon God. And so the man waits quietly for the dawn, and his whole soul is one absorbing desire that God may dwell with him and brighten and gladden him.

1. *That God may dwell with him.*

2. *That God may brighten and gladden him.*

IV. THE MISSIONARY CALL. Vss. 7-8.   L

A. The Extent of the Invitation.

1. *In his first cry the Psalmist was only interested in himself and God.* Vs. 1. There was no room for anything in his heart when he began this psalm except his own self in his misery and that Great One high above him. There was nobody in all the universe to him but himself and God, at his first cry from the depths.

2. *Now his interest extends to his fellow-men.* But there is nothing that so knits him to all his fellows and brings him into such wide-reaching bonds of amity and benevolence as the sense of God's forgiving mercy for his own soul. So the call bursts from the lips of the pardoned man, inviting all to taste the experience and exercise the trust which have made him glad: "Let Israel hope in the Lord."

B. The Content of the Invitation.

1. *There is plenteous redemption.* Vs. 7. Not only forgiveness, but redemption. It is "plenteous" — multiplied, as the word might be rendered.

2. *There is inexhaustible redemption.* Vs. 8. It is inexhaustible redemption, not to be provoked, not to be overcome by any obstinacy of evil — available for every grade and every repitition of transgression.

CONCLUSION

"With Him is plenteous redemption; He shall redeem Israel from all his iniquities." This is the Old Testament prophecy. Let me leave on your hearts the New Testament fulfilment of it. "Thou shalt call His name Jesus, for He shall save His people from their sins" (Matthew 1:21). That is the fulfilment, the vindication and explanation of the Psalmist's hope.

9

The Sluggard in Harvest

The sluggard will not plough by reason of the cold; therefore shall he beg in harvest and have nothing. —**Proverbs 20:4***

LIKE all the sayings of this book this is simply a piece of plain, practical common sense. It is intended to inculcate the lesson that men should diligently seize the opportunity whilst it is theirs. The sluggard is one of the pet aversions of the Book of Proverbs, which, unlike most other manuals of Eastern wisdom, has a profound reverence for honest work.

I. THE PRINCIPLES CRYSTALIZED IN THIS PICTURESQUE PROVERB.

A. Present Conduct Determines Future Conditions.

1. *This principle is true about life in general.* The position which a man fills, the tasks which he has to perform, and the whole host of things which make up the externals of his life, depend on far other conditions than any that he brings to them. But yet, on the whole, it is true that what a man does, and is, settles how he fares.

2. *This principle is especially true about youth.* You can, I was going to say, be anything you make up your minds to; and within reasonable limits, this bold saying is true. "Ask what thou wilt and it shall be given to thee" is what nature and Providence, almost as really as grace and Christ, say to every young man and woman.

B. The Easy Road is Generally the Wrong Road.

1. *The certainty of obstacles in the way of a noble life.* There are always obstacles in the way of a noble life. If a man is

---

*From *The Wearied Christ.*

going to be anything worth being or to do anything worth doing he must start with and adhere to the resolve "to scorn delights and live laborious days."

2. *The condition to be met in order to live a noble life.* Self-denial and rigid self-control, in its two forms, of stopping your ears to the attractions of lower pleasures and of cheerily encountering difficulties is an indispensable condition of any life which shall at last yield a harvest worth the gathering.

C. The Season Let Slip Is Gone Forever.

1. *The tragedy of lost opportunity.* Opportunity is bald behind and must be grasped by the forelock. Life is full of tragic might-have-beens. No regret, no remorse, no self-accusation, no clear recognition that I was a fool will avail one jot. "Too late" is the saddest of human words.

2. *The solemn admonition to faithful discharge of duties.* As the stages of our lives roll on, unless each is filled with the discharge of the duties and the appropriation of the benefits which it brings, then, to all eternity that moment will never return and the sluggard may beg in harvest that he may have the chance to plough once more, and have none.

II. THE APPLICATION OF THE PRINCIPLES CRYSTALIZED IN THE PICTURESQUE PROVERB.

A. The Application to Daily Secular Work.

1. *The necessity of hard work.* Do not trust to any way of getting on by dodges or speculation, or favor, or by anything but downright hard work. Don't shirk difficulties, don't try to put the weight of the work upon some colleague or other, that you may have an easier life of it.

2. *The blessing of work.* "In all labor there is profit." Whether the profit comes to you in the shape of advancement, position, promotion in your offices, partnerships perhaps, wealth and the like, or no, the profit lies in the work. Honest toil is the key to pleasure.

B. The Application to Intellectual Activity.

1. *The intellect is a gift of God.* Carry these principles with you in the cultivation of that important part of yourself — your intellects. Some of you, perhaps, are students by profession; I should like all of you to make a conscience of making the best of your brains, as God has given them to you in trust.

2. *Man's responsibility in the use of his intellect.* Amidst all the flood of feeble, foolish, flaccid literature with which we are afflicted at this day, I wonder how many of you ever set yourselves to some great book or subject that you cannot understand without effort. Unless you do you are not faithful stewards of God's gift of that great faculty which apprehends and lives upon truth.

C. The Application to the Formation of Character.

1. *Nobility of life is the result of toil and divine grace.* Nothing will come to you noble, great, or elevating in that direction unless it is sought, and sought with toil. Wisdom and truth and all their elevating effects upon human character absolutely require for their acquirement effort and toil.

2. *Character is formed during the impressionable years of life.* In the making of character we have to work as a painter in fresco does, with a swift brush on the plaster while it is wet. It sets and hardens in an hour. And men drift into habits which become tyrannies and dominant before they know where they are.

D. The Application to the Christian Life.

1. *The wisdom and necessity of beginning the Christian life at the earliest moment.* If you do not yield yourselves to Jesus Christ in your early days and take Him for your Savior and rest your souls upon Him and then take Him for your Captain and Commander, for your Pattern and Example, for your Companion and your Aim, you will lose what you can never make up by any future course.

2. *The present life in relation to the future.* This life as a whole is to the future life as the ploughing time is to the harvest and there are awful words in Scripture which seem to point in the same direction in reference to the irrevocable and irreversible issue of neglected opportunities on earth as this proverb does in regard to the ploughing and harvests of this life.

CONCLUSION

I dare not conceal what seems to me the New Testament confirmation and deepening of the solemn words of our text, "He shall beg in harvest and have nothing," by the Master's words, "Many shall say to Me in that day, Lord! Lord! and I will say, I never knew you." Now, while it is called day harden not your hearts.

10

The Charge of the Pilgrim Priests

*Watch ye, and keep them, until ye weigh
them . . . at Jerusalem, in the chambers of
the house of the Lord.* —Ezra 8:29*

THE little band of Jews returning from Babylon had
just started on a long pilgrimage and made a brief halt in order to
get everything in order for their transit across the desert; when
their leader, Ezra, taking count of his men, discovers that amongst
them there are none of the priests or Levites. He then takes
measures to reinforce his little army with a contingent of these
and entrusts to their care a very valuable treasure in gold and
silver and sacrificial vessels which had been given to them for
use in the house of the Lord.

I. THE PRECIOUS TREASURE.

A. **The Treasure of Ourselves.** The metaphor is capable of
two applications. The first is to the rich treasure and solemn
trust of our own nature, of our own souls; the faculties and
capacities, precious beyond all count, rich beyond all else that
a man has ever received. The precious treasure of your own
natures, your own hearts, your own understandings, wills,
consciences, desires — keep these until they are weighed in the
house of the Lord.

B. **The Treasure of the Gospel.** And in like manner, taking
the other aspect of the metaphor — we have given to us, in
order that we may do something with it, that great deposit
and treasure of truth, which is all embodied and incarnated
in Jesus Christ our Lord. It is bestowed upon us that we may

---

* From *Week-Day Evening Addresses.*

47

use it for ourselves and in order that we may carry it triumphantly all through the world. Possession involves responsibility always. It is given to us in order that we may keep it safe and carry it high up across the desert as becomes the priests of the most high God.

II. THE GUARDIANSHIP OF THE TREASURE.

"Watch ye, keep them." I cannot do more than touch upon two or three of the ways in which this charge may be worked out or in its application for ourselves.

A. Unslumbering Vigilance. First of all, no slumber; not a moment's relaxation; or some of those who lie in wait for us on the way will be down upon us and some of the precious things will go. While the rest of the wearied camp slept, the guardians of the treasure had to outwatch the stars. While others might straggle on the march, lingering here and there or resting on some patch of green, they had to close up round their precious charge; others might let their eyes wander from the path, they had ever to look to their care.

B. Lowly Trust. Ezra said in effect, "Not all the cohorts of Babylon can help us; and we do not want them. We have one strong hand that will keep us safe." His confidence was, "God will bring us all safe out to the end there and we shall carry every glittering piece of precious things that we brought out of Babylon right into the Temple of Jerusalem." "I know whom I have believed, and am persuaded that He is able to keep that which I have committed unto Him against that day" (II Timothy 1:12).

C. Punctilious Purity. "I said unto them, Ye are holy unto the Lord; the vessels are holy unto the Lord." It was fitting that the priests should carry the things that belonged to the Temple. To none other guardianship but the guardianship of the possessors of a symbolic and ceremonial purity could the vessels of a symbolic and ceremonial worship be entrusted; and to none others but the possessors of real and spiritual holiness can the treasures of the true Temple, of an inward and spiritual worship, be entrusted. The only way to keep our treasure undiminished and untarnished is to keep ourselves pure and clean.

D. Constant Use. Although the vessels which those priests bore through the desert were used for no service during all the weary march, they weighed just the same when they got to the end as at the beginning though, no doubt, even their fine gold had become dim and tarnished through disuse. But if we do no use the vessels that are entrusted to our care they will not weigh the same. Gifts that are used fructify. Capacities that are strained to the uttermost increase. Service strengthens the power of service.

III. THE ACCOUNTING OF THE TREASURE.

And lastly think of that weighing in the House of the Lord. Cannot you see the picture of the little band when they finally reach the goal of their pilgrimmage; and three days after they arrived, as the narrative tells us, went up into the Temple and there, by number and weight, rendered their charge and were clear of their responsibility?

A. The Encouragement of Anticipation of the Day of Accounting. Oh, how that thought of the day when they would empty out the rich treasure upon the marble pavement and clash the golden vessels into the scales, must have filled their hearts with vigilance during all the weary watches, when desert stars looked down upon the slumbering encampment and they paced wakeful all the night.

B. The Joy of Anticipation of the Day of Accounting. How the thought, too, must have filled their hearts with joy when they tried to picture to themselves the sigh of satisfaction and the sense of relief with which, after their perils, their "feet would stand within thy gates, O Jerusalem," and they would be able to say, "That which Thou has given me I have kept and nothing of it is lost."

CONCLUSION

Though it cannot be that you and I shall meet the trial and the weighing of that great day without many a flaw and much loss, yet we may say, "I know whom I have believed, and that He is able to keep my deposit — whether it be in the sense of that which I have committed unto Him, or in the sense of that which He has committed unto me — against that day." We may hope, that, by His gracious help and His pitying acceptance, even such careless stewards and negligent watchmen as we are, may lay ourselves down in peace at the last saying, "I have kept the faith"; and may be awakened by the word, "Well done, good and faithful servant."

11

The Joy of the Lord

The joy of the Lord is your strength.
— Nehemiah 8:10*

HERE, in the incident before us, there has come a time in Nehemiah's great enterprise, when the law, long forgotten, long broken by the captives, is now to be established again as the rule of the newly founded commonwealth. Naturally enough there comes a rememberance of many things in the past history of the people; and tears not unnaturally mingle with the thankfulness that again they are a nation, having a Divine worship and a Divine law in their midst. The leader of them, knowing for one thing that if the spirits of his people once began to flag, they could not face nor conquer the difficulties of their position, said to them, "Neither be ye sorry, for the joy of the Lord is your strength." And that is as true, brethren, with regard to us, as it ever was in these old times.

I. THE JOY OF THE LORD IS THE NATURAL RESULT OF CHRISTIAN FAITH.

A. The Gospel's Provision for Joy.

1. *The Gospel provides joy by what it brings.* It gives us what we well call a sense of acceptance with God, it gives us God for the rest of our spirits, it gives us the communion with Him which in proportion as it is real, will be still; and in proportion as it is still, will be all bright and joyful.

2. *The Gospel provides joy by what it takes away.* It takes away from us the fear that lies before us, the strifes that lie within us, the desperate conflict that is waged between

---

* From *Sermons Preached in Manchester,* First Series.

a man's conscience and his inclinations, between his will and his passions, which tears the heart asunder, and always makes sorrow and tumult wherever it comes. It takes away the sense of sin.

B. Sorrow is a Foundation Upon Which Rests the Joy of the Lord.

1. *The reason for the believer's sorrow.* If we think of what our faith does; of the light that it casts upon our condition, upon our nature, upon our responsibilities, upon our sins, and upon our destinies, we can easily see how, if gladness be one part of its operation, no less really and truly is sadness another.

2. *The importance of sorrow as a foundation for joy.* There is nothing more contemptible in itself, and there is no more sure mark of a trivial round of occupation than unshaded gladness, that rests on no deep foundations of quiet, patient grief; grief, because I know what I am and what I ought to be; grief, because I have learned the "exceeding sinfulness of sin"; grief, because, looking out upon the world, I see as other men do not see, hell-fire burning at the back of the mirth and the laughter, and know what it is that men are hurrying to.

3. *Joy and sorrow are not contradictory.* These two states of mind, both of them the natural operations of any deep faith, may co-exist and blend into one another, so that the gladness is sobered and chastened and made manly and noble; and that the sorrow is like some thunder-cloud all streaked with bars of sunshine that go into its deepest depths. The joy lives in the midst of the sorrow; the sorrow springs from the same root as the gladness.

II. THE JOY OF THE LORD IS A MATTER OF CHRISTIAN DUTY.

A. The Reasons Why It Is a Christian Duty.

1. *It is a commandment of God's Word.* It is a commandment here (Nehemiah 8:10) and it is a commandment in the New Testament (Philippians 4:4).

2. *The Christian can to a great extent regulate his emotions.* To rejoice in the Lord is a duty, a thing that the Apostle enjoins; from which, of course, it follows that somehow or other it is to a large extent within one's power and that even the indulgence in this emotion and the degree to which a Christian life shall be a cheerful life is dependent in a large measure on our own volitions and stands on the same footing as our obedience to God's other commandments.

3. *The Christian can determine his thoughts which regulate his emotions.* To lose thoughts of ourselves in God's truth about Himself is our duty.

B. The Hindrances to this Christian Duty.

1. *Temperament.* Some of us are naturally faint-hearted, timid, skeptical of any success, grave, melancholy, or hard to stir to any emotion. To such there will be an added difficulty in making quiet confident joy any very familiar guest in their home or in their place of prayer. But even such should remember that the "powers of the world to come," the energies of the Gospel, are given to us for the very express purpose of overcoming, as well as of hallowing natural dispositions.

2. *Deficiency in the depth and reality of our faith.* It is only where there is much faith and consequent love that there is much joy. If there is but small faith, there will not be much gladness.

3. *Failure to take the position a Christian has a right to take.* You must cast yourselves on God's Gospel with all your weight, without any hanging back, without any doubt, without even the shadow of a suspicion that it will give — that the firm, pure floor will give and let you through into the water.

III. THE JOY OF THE LORD IS A SOURCE OF STRENGTH.

A. It Affects Our Efficiency.

1. *Because man's force comes from his mind and not his body.* All gladness has something to do with our efficiency; for

it is the prerogative of man that his force comes from his mind and from his body.

2. *Because joy lightens work.* If we have souls at rest in Christ or the wealth and blessedness of a tranquil gladness lying there work will be easy.

3. *Because joy repels temptations.* If the soul is full, and full of joy, what side will be exposed to the assault of any temptation?

B. It Is Necessary to Effective Christian Service.

1. *The things which cannot strengthen a man.* No vehement resolutions, no sense of your own sinfulness, nor even contrite remembrance of past failures ever made a man strong.

2. *Joy is essential to strength.* For strength there must be joy.

3. *The most dangerous opponent to Christian work* — despondency and simple sorrow.

CONCLUSION

You are weak unless you are glad; you are not glad and strong unless your faith and hope are fixed in Christ and unless you are working from and not towards the assurance of salvation.

12

The Inhabitant of the Rock

Thou wilt keep him in perfect peace,
whose mind is stayed on Thee; because he
trusteth in Thee. Trust ye in the Lord
forever; for in the Lord Jehovah is ever-
lasting strength. — Isaiah 26:3, 4*

THERE is an obvious parallel between these verses and the two preceding ones. The safety which is there set forth as the result of dwelling in a strong city is here presented as the consequences of trust. The emblem of the fortified place passes into that of the Rock of Ages. In the two preceding verses we have the triumphant declaration of security followed by a summons to "open the gates," so here we have the declaration of perfect peace followed by a summons to "trust in the Lord forever."

I. THE NATURE OF TRUST.

A. **The Meaning of Trust Stated.** Now the literal meaning of the expression here rendered "to trust" is to lean upon anything. As we say, trust is reliance.

B. **The Meaning of Trust Illustrated and Applied.** As a weak man might stay his faltering, tottering steps upon some strong staff or might lean upon the outstretched arm of a friend, so we, conscious of our weakness, aware of our faltering feet, and realizing the roughness of the road and the smallness of our strength, may lay the whole weight of ourselves upon the loving strength of Jehovah.

---

* From *Paul's Prayers.*

55

II. THE STEADFAST PEACEFULNESS OF TRUST.

A. Trust Produces Steadfastness.

1. *Steadfastness is not a characteristic of the average man's life.* Most men's lives are blown about by winds of circumstance, directed by gusts of passion, shaped by accidents, and are fragmentary and jerky, like some ship at sea with nobody at the helm, heading here and there as the force of the wind or the flow of the current may carry them.

2. *Steadfastness is the result of trusting in God.* No man can steady his life except by clinging to a holdfast outside of himself. Some of us look for that stay in the fluctuations and fleetingnesses of creatures and some of us are wiser and saner and look for it in the steadfastness of the unchanging God. Only they who stay themselves upon God are steadfast and solid.

B. The Steadfast Mind is Kept of God.

1. *The necessity to have an attitude of confidence.* In order to receive the full blessed effects of trust into our characters and lives we must persistently and doggedly keep on in the attitude of confidence. There must be a steadfast working if there is to be a continual flow.

2. *The certainty that God keeps the steadfast mind in perfect peace.* It is the mind that cleaves to God which God keeps. I suppose there was floating before Paul's thought some remembrance of this great passage of the evangelical prophet when he said, "The peace of God which passeth understanding shall keep your hearts and minds through Christ Jesus" (Philippians 4:7). It is the steadfast mind that is kept in perfect peace.

C. The Steadfast Mind is Filled With Peace.

1. *The character of the peace.* There is something very beautiful in the prophet's abandoning the attempt to find any adjective which adequately characterizes the peace of which he has been speaking. He falls back upon an expedient which is a confession of the impotence of human speech

worthily to portray its subject when he simply says, "Thou shalt keep in peace, peace . . . because he trusteth in Thee." The reduplication expresses the depth and completeness of the tranquility which flows into the heart.

2. *The dependence of peace.* The possession of this deep, unbroken peace does not depend on the absence of conflict, distraction, trouble or sorrow, but on the presence of God.

III. THE WORTHINESS OF THE DIVINE NAME TO EVOKE AND THE POWER OF DIVINE CHARACTER TO REWARD THE TRUST.

A. The Meaning of the Words, "In the Lord Jehovah is Everlasting Strength.

1. *The literal translation of "everlasting strength."* The words feebly rendered in the Authorized Version "everlasting strength" are literally "the Rock of Ages."

2. The significance of "Lord Jehovah." Here we have the name of Jehovah reduplicated. In Jah Jehovah is the Rock of Ages. In adoration he contents himself with twice taking the name upon his lips in order to *impress* what he cannot *express,* the majesty and the sufficiency of that name.

B. The Truth Expressed by the Words "In the Lord Jehovah is Everlasting Strength."

1. *Jehovah is the unchangeable, self-existent, covenant keeping God.* Jehovah, in its grammatical signification, puts emphasis upon the absolute, underived and therefore unlimited, unconditioned, unchangeable, eternal being of God. "I Am that I Am" (Exodus 3:14). It is the name of the God who entered into covenant with His ancient people and remains bound by His covenant to bless us.

2. *The child of God has an unchangeable defence.* The metaphor needs no expansion. We understand that it conveys the idea of unchangeable defence. They who fasten themselves to that Rock are safe in its unchangeable strength. "The conies are a feeble folk, yet they make their houses in

the rocks" (Proverbs 30:26). So our weakness may house itself there and be at rest.

IV. THE SUMMONS TO TRUST.

A. **It is a Merciful Summons.** Surely, the blessed effects of trust, of which we have been speaking, have a voice of merciful invitation summoning us to exercise it. The promise of peace appeals to the deepest, though often neglected and misunderstood longings of the human heart. Storms live in the lower regions of the atmosphere; get up higher and there is peace.

B. **It is a Summons to Faith.** Surely the name of the Rock of Ages is an invitation to us to put our trust in Him. If a man knew God as He is, he could not choose but trust Him.

C. **It is a Summons Addressed to All.** It is a summons addressed to us all. "Trust ye" — whoever you are — "in the Lord forever."

CONCLUSION

When from the cross there comes to all our hearts the merciful invitation, "Believe on the Lord Jesus Christ, and thou shalt be saved" (Acts 16:31), why should not we each answer,

> "Rock of Ages, cleft for me,
> Let me hide myself in Thee"?

I will trust in the Lord
"song"

Christ our panacea
Satiry = Curative

13

Me with me lamb of God

A Three-fold Disease and a Two-fold Cure

> *I will cleanse them from all their iniquity,*
> *whereby they have sinned against Me; and*
> *I will pardon all their iniquities, whereby*
> *they have sinned, and whereby they have*
> *transgressed against Me.*— Jeremiah 33:8*

JEREMIAH was a prisoner in the palace of the last King of Judah. The long, national tragedy had reached almost the last scene of the last act. The prophet never faltered in predicting its fall, but he as uniformly pointed to a period behind the impelling ruin when all should be peace and joy. That fair vision of the future begins with the offer of healing and cure, and with the exuberant promise of my text.

I. A THREE-FOLD VIEW OF THE SAD CONDITION OF HUMANITY.

A. The Three Words Used by the Prophet to Describe the Sad Condition of Humanity. You see there are three expressions which roughly may be taken as referring to the same ugly fact, but yet not meaning quite the same—"iniquity, or iniquities, sin, transgression." These three all speak about the same sad element in your experience and mine, but they speak about it from somewhat different points of view, and I wish to try to bring out that difference for you.

1. *Iniquity.*

2. *Sin.*

3. *Transgression.*

---

* From *After the Resurrection.*

59

B. The Significance of the Three Words Used by the Prophet to Describe the Sad Condition of Humanity.

1. *A Sinful life is a twisted or warped life.* The word rendered "iniquity" in the Old Testiment in all probability literally means something that is not straight; that is, bent, or, as I said, twisted or warped. All sin is a twisting of the man from his proper course. Here is a straight road and there are the devious footpaths that we have made, many a coming back instead of going forward.

2. *A sinful life is a life that misses the mark.* The meaning of the word (sin) in the original is simply "that which misses the mark." There are two ways in which that thought may be looked at. Every wrong thing that we do misses the aim, if you consider what a man's aim ought to be. All godlessness, all the low, sinful lives that so many live, miss the shabby aim which they set before themselves.

3. *A sinful life is a rebellious life.* The expression which is translated in our text "transgressed," literally means "rebelled." And the lesson of it is, that all sin is, however little we think it, a rebellion against God. When we do wrong we lift up ourselves against our Sovereign King, and we say, "Who is the Lord that we should serve Him? Who is Lord over us? Let us break His bands asunder, and cast away His cords from us."

II. THE TWO-FOLD BRIGHT HOPE WHICH SHINES THROUGH THE DARKNESS.

If sin combines in itself all these characteristics that I have touched upon, then clearly there is guilt and clearly there are stains; and the gracious promise of this text deals with both the one and the other.

A Pardon.

1. *The meaning of pardon.* What do you fathers and mothers do when you forgive your child? You may use the rod or you may not. Forgiveness does not lie in letting him off the punishment; but forgiveness lies in the flowing to the

child, uninterrupted, of the love of the parent heart, and that is God's forgiveness. "Thou wast a God that forgavest them, though Thou tookest vengeance of their inventions" (Psalm 99:8).

2. *The need of pardon.* Do you need pardon? What does the sense of remorse say? What does conscience say? There are tendencies to ignore the fact that all sin must necessarily lead to tremendous consequences of misery. It does so in this world, more or less. A man goes into another world as he left this one and you and I believe — "after death, the judgment" (Hebrews 9:27).

3. *The basis of pardon.* "Himself bore our sins in His own body on the tree" (I Peter 2:24). Jesus Christ, the Son of God, died that the loving forgiveness of God might find its way to man's heart, whilst yet the righteousness of God remained untarnished. I know not any gospel that goes deep enough to touch the real sore place in human nature except the gospel that says, "Behold the Lamb of God that taketh away the sin of the world" (John 1:29). *Blood.*

fire *write* *Catharsis*

B. **Cleansing.** *Vastation obution,*

1. *The reason for cleansing.* But forgiveness is not enough, for the worst results of past sin are the habits of sin which it leaves within us; so that we all need cleansing.

2. *The impossibility of man to cleanse himself.* Can we cleanse ourselves? Let experience answer. Did you ever try to cure yourself of some little trick of gesture, or manner, or speech? And did you not find out then how strong the trivial habit was? You never know the force of a current till you try to row against it. "Can the Ethiopian change his skin?" (Jeremiah 13:23).

3. *The secret of cleansing.* So, again, we say that Jesus Christ who died for the remission of sins that are past, lives that He may give to each of us His own blessed life and power, and so draw us from our evil and invest us with His good.

his Vicarious death etc,

CONCLUSION

Pardon and cleansing are our two deepest needs. There is one hand from which we can receive them both, and one only. There is one condition on which we shall receive them, which is that we trust in Him "who was crucified for our offences" and lives to hallow us into His own likeness.

What a Friend we have in Jesus, "There is a Friend that ~~~~

14

A Pair of Friends

Can two walk together, except they be agreed?
— Amos 3:3*

THE "two" whom the prophet would see walking together are God and Israel and his question suggests not only the companionship and communion with God which are the highest form of religion and the aim of all forms and ceremonies of worship, but also the inexorable condition on which alone that height of communion can be secured and sustained. Two may walk together, though the one be God and the other be I. But they have to be agreed thus far, at any rate, that both shall wish to be together and both be ~~going~~ *Traveling* the same road.

I. THE POSSIBLE BLESSED COMPANIONSHIP WHICH MAY CHEER A LIFE.

A. Three Aspects of Divine Companionship.

1. *Walking before God* (Genesis 17:1). Sometimes we read about "walking before God," as Abraham was bid to do. That means ordering ~~the~~ daily life under the continued sense that we are "ever in the great Taskmaster's eye."

2. *Walking after God* (Deuteronomy 13:4). This means conforming the will and active efforts to the rule that He has laid down, setting our steps firm on the ~~paths~~ path that He has prepared that we should walk in ~~them~~ and accepting His providences. *Acknowledging the Lordship Almighty*

3. *Walking with God* (Genesis 5:22). High above both of these conceptions of a devout life is the one which is suggested by the text and was realized in the case of the

---

* From *The Victor's Crown.*

63

Satan is a Spoiler, infiltrator, Sabatoger etc he'll come between Friends, loose one etc.

patriarch Enoch — walking "with God." To "walk with Him" implies a constant, quiet sense of His divine presence which forbids loneliness, guides and defends, floods the soul and fills the life.

B. The Possibility of Divine Companionship.

1. *The certainty of its possibility.* Far above us as such experience seems to sound, such a life is a possibility for everyone of us. We may be able to say, as truly as our Lord said it, "I am not alone, for the Father is with Me" (John 16:32).

2. *The necessary requirement.* It is possible that the dreariest solitude of a soul may be turned into blessed fellowship with Him. But that solitude will not be so turned unless it is first painfully felt. We need to feel in our deepest hearts that loneliness on earth before we walk with God.

C. The Blessings of Divine Companionship.

1. *It results in mutual communications.* If we are so walking it is no piece of fanaticism to say that there will be mutual communications. As two friends on the road will interchange remarks about trifles and if they love each other, the remarks about trifles will be weighed with love, so we can tell our smallest affairs to God.

2. *It is the secret of all blessedness.* It is the only thing that will make a life absolutely sovereign over sorrow and fixedly unperturbed by all tempests and invulnerable to all "the slings and arrows of outrageous fortune."

II. THE SADLY INCOMPLETE REALITY IN MUCH CHRISTIAN EXPERIENCE WHICH CONTRASTS WITH THIS POSSIBILITY.

A. The Failure of Many Christians.

1. *To be habitually conscious of divine companionship.* I am afraid that very, very few so-called Christian people habitually feel, as they might do, the depth and blessedness of this communion.

2. *To actually have unbroken Divine companionship.* ~~And sure I am~~ that only a very small percentage of us have anything like the continuity of companionship which the text suggests as possible. Is it a line in my life or is there but a dot here and a dot there and long breaks between? The long embarrassed pauses in a conversation between two who do not know much of, or care much for, each other ~~are only too like~~ what occurs in many professing Christians' intercourse with God.

B. **A Description of the Failure of Many Christians.**

It is broken at the best, and imperfect at the completest, and shallow at the deepest.

1. *Broken companionship.*

2. *Imperfect companionship.*

3. *Shallow companionship.*

III. THE EXPLANATION OF THE FAILURE TO REALIZE THE LORD'S CONTINUAL PRESENCE.

A. **Failure of Agreement.** The two are not agreed; and that is why they are not walking together.

1. *The sensitiveness of the consciousness of God's presence.* The consciousness of God's presence with us is a very delicate thing. It is like a sensitive thermometer which will drop when an iceberg is a league off over the sea and scarcely visible.

2. *The reason for the failure of agreement.* We do not wish His company, or we are not in harmony with His thoughts, or we are not ~~going~~ His road and therefore, ~~of course~~, we part.

B. **Sin.**

1. *This is the primary factor.* ~~At~~ bottom there is only one thing that separates a soul from God, and that is sin — sin of some sort, like tiny grains of dust that get between two

polished plates in an engine, that ought to move smoothly and closely against each other. The obstruction may be invisible and yet be powerful enough to cause friction which hinders the working of the engine and throws everything out of gear.

2. *It may be that the ~~the~~ Christian ~~is~~ unconscious of it.* A light cloud that we cannot see may come between us and a star, and we shall only know it is there because that star is not visibly there. Similarly, many a Christian, quite unconsciously, has something ~~or other~~ in his habits or in his conduct or in his affections which would reveal itself to him, if he would look, as being wrong, because it blots out God. There may be scarcely any consciousness of parting company at the beginning. Let the man travel on upon it far enough and the two will be so far apart that he cannot see God or hear Him speak.

CONCLUSION

If we have parted from our Friend there should be no time lost ~~ere we go~~ back. May it be true of us that we walk with God, so that ~~at last~~ the great promise may be fulfilled about us, "that we shall walk with Him in white" being by His love accounted "worthy," and so "follow" and keep company with "the Lamb whithersoever He goeth."

"Draw near unto God"

If you no longer have love or a doctrine, or concern for your church you may not be walking with him "for he that saith that he walk with him — "if we walk in the light —"

15

Bartimaeus

> ... *Blind Baritmaeus, the son of Timaeus,*
> *sat by the highway side begging.*
> —Mark 10:46 (Read Mark 10:46-52)*

THE narrative of this miracle is contained in all the three first gospels. Mark's account is evidently that of an eye-witness. It is full of little particulars which testify thereto. Whether Bartimaeus had a companion or not, he was obviously the chief actor and spokesman. And the whole story seems to me to lend itself to the enforcement of some very important lessons, which I will try to draw from it.

I. THE BEGGAR'S PETITION AND THE ATTEMPTS TO SILENCE IT. Vss. 47-48.

A. The Beggar's Cry.

1. *It expresses an insight into Christ's place and dignity.* He cried, "Jesus, Thou Son of David," distinctly recognizing our Lord's Messianic character, His power and authority, and on that power and authority he built a confidence. He is sure of both the power and the will.

2. *It expresses a sense of need.* He individualizes himself, his need, Christ's power and willingness to help him.

3. *It expresses an insight into our Lord's unique character and power.* Unless we know Him to be all that is involved in that august title, "the son of David," I do not think our cries to Him will ever be very earnest.

B. The Attempts To Stifle The Beggar's Cry.

1. *The people, undoubedly, considered their efforts to stifle the cry a defense of the Master's dignity.*

---

* From *Triumphant Certainties.*

2. *The people were ignorant of the fact that the cry of wretchedness was sweeter to the Lord than the shallow hallelujahs.*

3. *The people failed to stifle the beggar's cry.* The more they silenced him, the more a great deal he cried.

II. CHRIST'S CALL AND THE SUPPLIANT'S RESPONSE. Vss. 49-50.

A. The Call of the Savior.

1. *The setting of the Savior's call.* He was on His road to His cross and the tension of spirit which the evangelist's notice as attaching to Him then and which filled the disciples with awe as they followed Him, absorbed Him, no doubt, at this hour so that He heard but little of the people's shouts.

2. *The interest of the Savior in the beggar.* But He did hear the blind beggar's cry and He arrested His march in order to attend to it.

3. *The present interest of the Savior in the cries of the needy.* The living Christ is as tender a friend, has as quick an ear, is as ready to help at once, today, as He was when outside the gate of Jericho. Christ still hears and answers the cry of need.

B. The Response of the Suppliant. Notice the suppliant's response. That is a very characteristic right-about-face of the crowd, who one moment were saying, "Hold your tongue and do not disturb Him," and the next moment were all eager to encumber him with help, and to say, "Rise up! Be of good cheer; He calleth thee." And what did the man do?

1. *The beggar arose.* "Sprang to his feet" — as the word rightly rendered would be.

2. *The beggar flung away his garment.* And flung away his disordered and offensive rags that he had wrapped round him for warmth and softness of seat, as he waited at the gate.

3. *The beggar came to Jesus.* Brethren, "casting aside every weight and the sin that doth so easily beset us; let us run" to the same Refuge (Heb. 2:1).

III. THE QUESTION OF ALL-GRANTING LOVE AND THE ANSWER OF CONSCIOUS NEED. Vs. 51.

A. The Interrogation.

1. *The meaning of the question.* It was the implicit pledge that whatever he desired he should receive.

2. *The reason for the question.* Jesus knew that the thing this man wanted was the thing that He delighted to give.

3. *The authority of the Questioner.* Think of a man doing as Jesus Christ did — standing before another and saying, "I will give you anything that you want." He must be either a madman, or a blasphemer, or "God manifest in the flesh"; Almighty power guided by infinite love.

B. The Response.

1. *The content of the answer.* He had no doubt what he wanted most — the opening of those blind eyes of his.

2. *It was the answer of a wise man.* If you are a wise man, if you know yourself and Him, your answer will come as swiftly as the beggar's — Lord! heal me of my blindness and take away my sin and give me Thy salvation.

3. *Man's greatest need is expressed in the answer.*

IV. SIGHT GIVEN AND THE RECEIVER FOLLOWING. Vs. 52.

A. The Gift of Sight.

1. *The cure was in answer to the beggar's cry.* Bartimaeus had scarcely ended speaking when Christ began. He was blind at the beginning of Christ's little sentence; he saw at the end of it.

2. *The cure was immediate.* The answer came instantly and the cure was as immediate as the movement of Christ's heart in answer.

3. *The immediateness of salvation.* As soon as we desire we have and as soon as we have we see.

B. THE CONDITION BY WHICH CHRIST'S MERCY RUSHES INTO A MAN'S SOUL.

1. *Faith made it possible for Christ's power to make the beggar whole.* Here we have a clear statement of the path by which Christ's mercy rushes into a man's soul. "Thy faith hath saved thee" (vs. 52).

2. *Physical miracles do not always require trust in Christ but the possession of Christ's salvation does.*

CONCLUSION

Now, all this story should be the story of each one of us. One modification we have to make upon it, for we do not need to cry persistently for mercy, but to trust in, and to take, the mercy that is needed. One other difference there is between Bartimaeus and many of my hearers. He knew what he needed, and some of you do not. But Christ is calling us all and my business now is to say to each of you . . ., "Rise! be of good cheer; He calleth thee."

16

How the Little May Be Used
to Get the Great

> *He that is faithful in that which is least is
> faithful also in much, and he that is unjust
> in the least is unjust also in much. If,
> therefore, ye have not been faithful in the
> unrighteous mammon, who will commit to
> your trust the true riches? And if ye have
> not been faithful in that which is another
> man's, who shall give you that which is
> your own?* — Luke 16:10-12*

THESE are very revolutionary words in more than one aspect. There are two things remarkable about them. One is the contrast which is seen in all three verses between what our Lord calls "mammon" (that is, simply outward good) and the inward riches of a heart devoted to and filled with God and Christ. But another striking thing about the words is the broad, bold statement that a man's use of the lower goods determines, or is at least an element in determining his possession of the highest.

I. A NEW STANDARD OF VALUE.

A. The Antithesis Between "Small" and "Great." (Vs. 10).

1. *They imply a comparison with each other.*

2. *They imply a common standard of value for both.* "Small" and "Great," of course, are relative terms; they imply a comparison with each other, and imply also a reference of both to a common standard of value.

---

* From *A Year's Ministry*, Second Series.

3. *The common standard of value stated.* What are these two classes of good measured by, but their respective power of filling the heart.

B. **The Antithesis Between "Unrighteous Mammon" and the "True Riches." Vs. 11.**

1. *The meaning of "unrighteous."* If we keep strictly to the antithesis, "unrighteous" must be the opposite of "true." The word would then come to mean very nearly the same as deceitful, that which betrays.

2. *The deception of material good.* No man ever found in any outward good, when he got it, that which he fancied was in it when he was chasing after it.

3. *The true riches.* But the inward riches of faith, true holiness, lofty aspirations, Christ centered purposes, all these are true. They bring more than they said they would.

C. **The Antithesis Between "Another's" and "Your Own." Vs. 12.**

1. *The term "another's" may signify stewardship.* Another's? Well, that may mean God's; and therefore you are stewards, as the whole parable that precedes the text has been teaching.

2. *The term "another's" implies the limitations and defects of outward possessions of outward good.* There is no real possession, even while there is an apparent one . . . . the possession is transcient as well as incomplete.

3. *The term "another's" suggests that accidents of life rob men of outward possessions.* What can be taken out of man's hands by death has no right to be called his. Each, for the moment says "Mine!' and Christ says "No! No! Another's!"

4. *The term "your own" refers to the things we are.* That which is your own is that which you can gather into your heart and keep there, and which death cannot take away from you.

II. THE HIGHEST USE OF THE LOWEST GOOD.

A. The Essence of the Principle. Vss. 10-12.

1. *The statement of the principle.* Our Lord . . . distinctly asserts here, as a principle, that our manner of employing the lesser goods of outward possessions is an element in determining the amount of our possession of the highest blessing.

2. *The Christian's fear concerning this principle* . . . Good people are sometimes cautious of asserting that with the plain emphasis with which it is here asserted, for fear they should damage the central truth that God's mercy and the gifts of His grace come to men through faith, not through their conduct.

3. *The necessity of faith in receiving the "true riches"* . . . A man receives into his heart "the true riches" simply on condition of his desiring them and of his trusting Jesus Christ to give them.

B. Conduct May Help or Hinder a Man in the Possession and Exercise of Faith.

1. *This does not militate against the central truth of the Gospel.*

2. *The love of the world a hindrance to salvation.* There are plenty of people . . . who are kept from being Christians because thy love the world too much.

3. *The love of the world a hindrance to Christians.* And is it not true about many Christians that their too high estimate of, and too great carefulness about, and too niggardly disposal of . . . the goods of this lesser life, are hindering their Christian career?

C. The Principle of the World and the Principle of Christ Contrasted.

1. *The principle of the world stated.* The world thinks that the highest use of the highest things is to gain possession of the lowest thereby. . .

2. *The principle of Christ stated.* Christ's teaching of the
relationship is exactly the opposite, that all the outward is
then lifted to its noblest purpose when it is made rigidly
subordinate to the highest . . .

III. THE FAITHFULNESS WHICH UTILIZES THE LOWEST AS A MEANS OF POSSESSING MORE FULLY THE HIGHEST.

You will be "faithful" if,
through all your administration of your possessions there
run the principles of stewardship, sacrifice, and brotherhood.

A. Stewardship.

1. *Consciousness of stewardship a requisite to faithfulness.* "Of
thine own have we given thee" (I Chron. 29:14) is to be
always our conviction, for all is God's . . .

2. *The obligation of stewardship.* One of the plainest duties
of stewardship is that we bring conscience and deliberate
consideration to bear upon our administration of this
world's goods.

3. *The extent of stewardship* — personal and domestic ex-
penditure, savings, and gifts.

B. Sacrifice.

1. *It is a fundamental law of the Christian life.*

2. *It must be applied in the region of outward possessions* . . .
It must be applied especially in his region of outward
possession where the opposite law of selfishness works most
strongly.

3. *It is based on God's mercies.*

C. Brotherhood.

1. *The Christian's obligation to share blessings with fellow-
believers* . . . It and they and we all belong to God.·

2. *The reason for the obligation to share blessings.* We get
everything in order that we may transmit it to others.

3. *The sphere of blessings shared,* outward goods, faculties of the mind and heart, wisdom, sympathy, the gifts of the Gospel.

CONCLUSION

Here and now we may win a greater possession of the love and likeness of God, and may have our spirits widened to receive more of all that makes us noble and calm, hopeful and strong, by our Christian administration of earthly goods. It will make us more capable of a larger possession of the life and the grace of God hereafter.

17

The Translation of Elijah
and the Ascension of Christ

> *And it came to pass, as they still went on,
> and talked, that, behold, there appeared a
> chariot of fire, and horses of fire, and
> parted them both asunder; and Elijah
> went up by a whirlwind into heaven.*
> — II Kings 2:11
>
> *And it came to pass, while He blessed
> them, He was departed from them, and
> carried up into heaven.* — Luke 24:51*

I COULD wish no better foil for the history of the ascension than the history of Elijah's rapture. The comparison rings out contrasts at every step, and there is no readier way of throwing into strong relief the meaning and purpose of the former than holding up beside it the story of the latter.

I. THE CONTRAST BETWEEN THE MANNER OF ELIJAH'S TRANSLATION AND THE MANNER OF OUR LORD'S ASCENSION.

A. The Manner of Elijah's Translation.

1. *It was a tempestuous translation.* The prophet's end was like the man. It was fitting that he should be swept up the skies in tempest and fire. The impetuosity of his nature and the stormy energy of his career had already been symbolized (I Kings 19:11-12).

2. *It was a translation by external power.* It suggests very plainly that Elijah was lifted to the skies by power acting on him from without. He did not ascend; he was carried

---

* From *The Secret of Power.*

up; the earthly frame and the human nature had no power to rise.

B. The Ascension of Christ.

1. *It was quiet.* The silent gentleness, which did not strive nor cry nor cause His voice to be heard in the streets, marks Him even in that hour of lofty and transcendent triumph. No blaze of fiery chariots nor agitation of tempest is needed to bear Him heavenwards.

2. *It was by inherent power.* Our Lord's ascension by His own inherent power is brought into boldest relief when contrasted with Elijah's rapture and is evidently the fitting expression, as it is the consequence, of His sole and singular Divine nature.

II. THE CONTRAST BETWEEN THE LIFE'S WORK OF EACH WHICH PRECEDED THE TWO EVENTS.

A. Elijah Leaves His Work Unfinished.

1. *The symbol of transference.* The falling mantle of Elijah has become a symbol known to all the world for the transference of unfinished tasks and the appointment of successors to departed greatness. It was the symbol of office and authority transferred.

2. *The powerlessness of Elijah to make the transference.* Elisha asked that he might have a double portion of his master's spirit, not twice as much as his master, but the eldest son's share of the father's possessions. His master had no power to bestow the gift and had to reply as one who has nothing that he has not received and cannot dispose of the grace that dwells in him.

B. Christ Completes His Work. None are hailed as His successors. He has left no unfinished work which another may perfect. He has done no work which another may do again for new generations.

1. *He has no successors.*

2. *His work needs no repitition.*

III. THE TWO EVENTS CONTRASTED IN RELA-
TION TO THE TRANSITION TO A CONTIN-
UOUS ENERGY FOR AND IN THE WORLD.

A. **The Translation of Elijah Was Not a Transition to a
Continuous Energy for and in the World.** Clearly the
narrative derives all its pathos from the thought that Elijah's
work is done. His task is over and nothing more is to be
hoped for from him.

1. *His work was over.*

2. *Nothing more is to be hoped from him.*

B. **The Ascension of Christ Was a Transition to a Continuous Energy for and in the World.**

1. *The ascension of Christ did not end His activity for men,
but cast it in a new form.* When He ascended up on high
He relinquished nothing of His activity for us, but only
cast it into a new form which in some sense is yet higher
than that which it took on earth.

2. *The nature of Christ's present activity.* He works with His
servants. He has gone up to sit at the right hand of God.
The session at God's right hand means the repose of a perfected salvation, the communion of divine worship, the
exercise of all the omnipotence of God, the administration
of the world's history.

IV. THE TWO EVENTS CONTRASTED AS TO THE
BEARING ON THE HOPES OF HUMANITY
FOR THE FUTURE.

A. **Elijah's Translation in Relation to the Prophets.**

1. *It gave them a deepened conviction of Elijah's mission and
perhaps a clearer faith in the future life.* The prophet is
caught up to the glory and the rest for himself alone, and
the sole share which the gazing follower or sons of the

prophets had in his triumph was a deepened conviction of this prophet's mission and perhaps some clearer faith in a future life.

2. *It did not shed any light on their future.* No light streamed from it on their own future. The path they had to tread was still a common road into the great darkness, as solitary and unknown as before.

B. Christ's Ascension in Relation to Man.

1. *It assures the child of God of presence with Him.* His resurrection assures us that "them which sleep in Jesus will God bring with him" (I Thess. 4:14). His passage to the heaven assures us that "they who are alive and remain shall be caught up together with them" (I Thessalonians 4:17), and that all of both companies shall with Him live and reign, sharing His dominion, and molded to His image.

2. *It assures us of Christ's personal return.* "Ye men of Galilee, why stand ye gazing up into heaven? This same Jesus, which is taken up from you into heaven, shall so come in like manner as ye have seen Him go into heaven" (Acts 1:11). "So" — that is to say, personally, corporeally, on clouds, "and His feet shall stand in that day upon the Mount of Olives" (Zechariah 14:4).

CONCLUSION

That parting on Olivet cannot be the end. Such a leaving is the prophecy of happy greetings and an inseparable reunion. So let us take our share in the great joy with which the disciples returned to Jerusalem, left like sheep in the midst of wolves as they were, and "let us set our affections on things above, where Christ is, sitting at the right hand of God."

18

The Cross, the Glory of Christ and God

> *Therefore, when he was gone out, Jesus said, "Now is the Son of Man glorified, and God is glorified in Him. If God be glorified in Him, God shall also glorify Him in Himself, and shall straightway glorify Him.*   — John 13:31, 32*

IN immediate connection with the departure of the traitor comes this singular burst of triumph in our text. What Judas went to do was the beginning of Christ's glorifying. We have here, then, a triple glorification — the Son of Man glorified in His cross; God glorified in the Son of Man; and the Son of Man glorified in God.

I. THE SON OF MAN GLORIFIED IN HIS CROSS.

A. Christ's Two-fold Attitude Toward the Cross.

1. *The innocent shrinking of His manhood.* On the one hand we mark in Him an unmistakable shrinking from the cross, the innocent shrinking of His manhood expressed in such words as "I have a baptism to be baptized with, and how am I straitened till it be accomplished" (Luke 12:50); and in such incidents as the agony in Gethsemane.

2. *The triumphant anticipation.* And yet, side by side with that, not overcome by it, but not overcoming it, there is the opposite feeling, the reaching out almost with eagerness to bring the cross nearer to Himself.

---

* From *A Year's Ministry*, Second Series.

B. The Two-fold Manner in Which the Cross Glorified Christ.

1. *It was the revelation of His heart.* All His life long He
had been trying to tell the world how much He loved it. His
love had been, as it were, filtered by drops through His
words, through His deeds, through His whole demeanor
and bearing; but in His death it comes in a flood and pours
itself upon the world.

2. *It was the throne of His saving power.* The paradoxical
words of our text rest upon His profound conviction that
in His death He was about to put forth a mightier and
Diviner power than ever He had manifested in His life.
They are the same in effect and in tone as the great words:
"I, if I am lifted up, will draw all men unto Me" (John
12:32).

II. GOD GLORIFIED IN THE SON OF MAN.

A. The Glorification of God in the Cross of Christ.

1. *The indwelling of God in Christ.* God was in Christ in some
singular and emminent manner. If all His life was a continual manifestation of the Divine character, if Christ's
words were the Divine wisdom, if Christ's compassion was
the Divine pity, if Christ's loveliness was the Divine gentleness, if His whole human life and nature were the brightest
and cleanest manifestation to the world of what God is, we
can understand that the cross was the highest point of the
revelation of the Divine nature to the world.

2. *The death of Christ was substitutionary.* The words involve as it seems to me, not only that idea of a close, unique
union and indwelling of God in Christ, but they involve
also this other: that the sufferings bore no relation to the
deserts of the Person who endured them. "God was in
Christ reconciling the world to Himself" (II Cor. 5:19).

B. God is Glorified in the Cross of Christ Because it is a
Revelation of His Love.

1. *It is the greatest revelation of God's love.* The cross upon
which Christ died towers above all other revelations as the

most awful, the most sacred, the most tender, the most complete, the most heart-touching, the most soul-subduing manifestation of the Divine nature.

2. *It is the revelation which has brought the greatest blessing to men.* Has it not scattered doubts that lay like mountains of ice upon man's heart? Has it not swept the heavens clear of clouds that wrapped it in darkness?

III. THE SON OF MAN GLORIFIED IN THE FATHER.

A. The Nature of the Glorification.

1. *The statement of the glorification of the Son of Man in the Father.* "He shall also glorify Him in Himself" (vs. 32).

2. *The explanation of statement of the glorification of the Son of Man in the Father.* Mark that — "in Himself." That is the obvious antithesis to what has been spoken about in the previous clause, a glorifying which consisted in a manifestation to the external universe, whereas this is a glorifying within the depths of the Divine nature. And the best commentary upon it is our Lord's own words: "Father! glorify Thou Me with the glory which I had with Thee before the world was" (John 17:5).

B. The Person of the Glorification.

1. *It is the Son of Man.* That is to say, the Man Christ Jesus, "bone of our bone and flesh of our flesh," the very Person that walked upon earth and dwelt amongst us. . .

2. *It is the Son of Man incorporated into the heart of God.* He is taken up into the heart of God and in His manhood enters into that same glory which from the beginning the Eternal Word had with God.

C. The Time of the Glorification.

1. *It began in Paradise.* We have the glorifying set forth as commencing immediately upon the completion of God's glorifying by Christ upon the cross. "He shall straightway glorify Him" (Vs. 32). It began in that Paradise into which we know that upon that day He entered.

2. *It was manifested to the world at the resurrection and the ascension.* It was manifested to the world when He raised Him from the dead and gave Him glory. It reached a still higher point when they brought Him near unto the Ancient of Days.

3. *It will be more fully manifested at the second coming of Christ.* It shall rise to its highest manifestation before an assembled world when He shall come in His glory.

CONCLUSION

This, then, was the vision that lay before the Christ in that upper room, the vision of Himself glorified in His extreme shame because His cross manifested His love and His saving power; of God glorified in Him above all other of His acts of manifestation when He died on the cross, and revealed the very heart of God; and of Himself glorified in the Father when, exalted high above all creatures, He sitteth upon the Father's throne and rules the Father's realms.

19

The True Vision of the Father

> *Philip said unto Him, Lord, show us the
> Father, and it sufficeth us. Jesus said unto
> him, "Have I been so long time with you,
> and yet hast thou not known Me, Philip?
> He that hath seen Me hath seen the
> Father; and how sayest thou then, show
> us the Father? Believest thou not that I
> am in the Father, and the Father in Me?
> The words that I speak unto you I speak
> not of Myself: but the Father that dwel-
> leth in Me, He doeth the works. Believe
> Me that I am in the Father, and the Father
> in Me: or else believe Me for the very
> work's sake.* — John 14:8-11*

THE vehement burst with which Philip interrupts
the calm flow of our Lord's discourse is not the product of
mere frivolity or curiosity. As an Old Testament believer he
knew that Moses had once led the elders of Israel up to the
mount where "they saw the God of Israel," and to many
others had been granted sensible manifestations of the Divine
presence. His petition is childlike in its simplicity, beautiful
in its trust, noble and true in its estimate of what men need.
He longs to see God. He believes that Christ can show God;
he is sure that the sight of God will satisfy the heart.

I. THE REVELATION OF GOD IN CHRIST IS SUF-
FICIENT TO ANSWER MEN'S LONGINGS.
Vss. 8-9.

A. All Men Need a Visible Revelation of God.

1. *The history of heathendom shows us this need.* In every

---

* From *The Holy of Holies.*

84

land men have said, "The gods have come down to us in the likeness of men."

2. *The cultured have the same need.* The highest cultivation of this highly cultivated self-conscious century, has not removed men from the same necessity that the rudest savage has, to have some kind of manifestation of the divine nature other than the dim and vague ones which are possible apart from the revelation of God in Christ.

3. *The whole world has this need.*

4. *It is a personal need.* Your heart and mind require it.

B. **Man's Need of a Visible Revelation of God is Met in Christ.**

1. *Abstract qualities are made visible through the deeds of the body.* Wisdom, love, purity, are only seen through the deeds of the body.

2. *The invisible God is made visible through the incarnate Christ.* He is the manifestation to the world of the unseen Father.

C. **The Revelation of God in Christ is Sufficient for Man.** If we can see God it suffices us. Then the mind settles down upon the thought of Him as the basis of all being, and of all change; and the heart can twine itself round Him, and the seeking soul folds its wings and is at rest; and the troubled spirit is quiet, and the accusing conscience is silent, and the rebellious will is subdued.

1. *It is sufficient for the mind.*

2. *It is sufficient for the heart.*

3. *It is sufficient for the will.*

II. **THE REVELATION OF GOD IN CHRIST IS MADE POSSIBLE BY THE DIVINE AND MUTUAL INDWELLING OF THE FATHER AND THE SON. Vs. 10.**

A. Christ's Claim to the Oneness of Unbroken Commission.

1. *"I am in the Father"* indicates the suppression of all independent and therefore rebellious will, consciousness, thought and action.

2. *"The Father in Me"* indicates the influx into that perfectly filial manhood of the whole fulness of God in unbroken, continuous, gentle, deep flow.

B. Christ's Claim to Oneness of Complete Cooperation.

1. *Correspondence of statements.* "The words that I speak unto you, I speak not of Myself" corresponds to "I am in the Father." "The Father that dwelleth in Me, He doeth the works" corresponds to "The Father in Me."

2. *The teaching of the corresponding statements.* The two put together teach us this, that by reason of that mysterious and ineffable union of communion, Jesus Christ in all His words and works is the perfect instrument of the Divine will.

C. Consideration Drawn From Christ's Two-Fold Claim.

1. *No deflection or disharmony between Christ and the Father.* Everything that Jesus Christ said He knew it to be God's speaking; everything that He did He knew it to be God's acting.

2. *A testimony to Christ's deity.* If Jesus had this consciousness (i.e., the oneness of unbroken communion and the oneness of complete cooperation) either He was mistaken and untrustworthy, or He is what the Church in all ages confessed Him to be, "the Everlasting Son of the Father."

III. THE REVELATION OF GOD IN CHRIST AND HIS UNION WITH GOD IS THE BASIS OF THE INVITATION TO BELIEVE IN CHRIST. Vs. 11.

A. Faith is the Bond of Union Between Men and Jesus Christ. Faith really is the outgoing of the whole man — heart, will, intellect, and all — to a person whom its grasps.

B. **Faith is Seeing and Knowing.** Philip said, "Show us the Father." Christ answers, "Believe, and thou dost see." The true way to knowledge and to a better vision than the uncertain vision of the eye is faith. In certitude and directness the knowledge of God that we have through faith in the Christ whom our eyes have never seen is far ahead of the certitude and the directness that attach to our mere bodily sight.

C. **Faith Based on Lower Grounds than the Highest is Faith and is Acceptable to God.** "Or else believe Me for the very works sake."

1. *The highest ground of faith is the image of Christ obliging man to trust Him.*

2. *The lower ground of faith is the works of Christ.* The "works" are mainly, though not exclusively, His miracles. If so, we are here taught that if a man has not come to that point of spiritual susceptibility in which the image of Jesus Christ lays hold upon his heart and obliges him to trust Him, and to love Him, there are yet the miracles to look at; and the faith that grasps them, and by help of that ladder climbs to Him, though it be second best, is yet real.

CONCLUSION

To each of us Christ addresses His merciful invitations, "Believe Me that I am in the Father, and the Father in Me." May we all answer, "We believe that Thou art the Christ, the Son of the living God!"

20

Witnesses of the Resurrection

> *Wherefore of these men which have companied with us all the time that the Lord Jesus went in and out among us . . . must one be ordained to be a witness of His resurrection.*
> — Acts 1:21-22*

THE words of the text are the Apostle Peter's own description of what was the office of an apostle — "to be a witness with us of Christ's resurrection." And the statement branches out into three considerations. First, we have here the witnesses; secondly, we have the sufficiency of their testimony; thirdly, we have the importance of the fact to which they bear their witness.

I. THE WITNESSES.

A. Their Qualification. The qualifications are only personal knowledge of Jesus Christ in His earthly history, because the function is only to attest His resurrection.

B. Their Function.

1. *Their work during Christ's earthly ministry.* The work of the apostles in Christ's lifetime embraced three elements, none of which were peculiar to them — to be with Christ, to preach, and to work miracles.

2. *Their work after Christ's ascension.* Their characteristic work after His ascension was witness bearing.

II. THE SUFFICIENCY OF THE TESTIMONY.

---

* From *Sermons Preached in Manchester*, Third Series.

A. **The Method of Establishing an Historical Fact:** the personal testimony of an eye witness. The way to establish a fact is only one — that is, to find somebody that can say, "I know it, for I saw it."

B. **The Character of the Testimony to the Resurrection.**

1. *The testimony of the Pauline epistles written not later than a quarter of a century after the resurrection.* The dates assigned to the four epistles — Romans, First and Second Corinthians and Galatians — by anybody, believer or unbeliever bring them within twenty-five years of the alleged date of Christ's resurrection. We find in all of them reference to the resurrection.

2. *The testimony of Paul's vision of the risen Christ ten years after the resurrection.* There is the reference to his own vision of the risen Savior (I Corinthians 15:8) which carries us up within ten years of the alleged fact. So, then, by the evidence of admittedly genuine documents which are dealing with the state of things ten years after the supposed resurrection there was a unanimous concurrence of belief on the part of the whole primitive church, so that even the heretics could be argued with on the ground of their belief in Christ's resurrection.

C. **The Implications of the Testimony of the Resurrection.**

1. *The statement of the implications.* If the resurrection be not a fact, then that belief was either a delusion or a deceit.

2. *The impossibility of the implications.* Not a delusion, for such an illusion is altogether unexampled; and it is absurd to think of it as being shared by a multitude like the early church. This is not a fond imagination giving an apparent substance to its own creation, but sense recognizing first the fact, "He is dead," and then, in opposition to expectation and when hope had sickened to despair, recognizing the astounding fact, "He liveth that was dead."

Not deceit. For the character of the men, and the characters of the associated morality, and the obvious absence of all self-interest, and the persecutions and sorrows which

they endured, make it inconceivable that the fairest building
that ever has been reared in the world, and which is
cemented by men's blood, should be built upon the mud and
slime of conscious deceit!

III. THE IMPORTANCE OF THE FACT.

**A. With the Resurrection of Jesus Christ Stands or Falls the
Deity of Christ.**

1. *The declaration of the Scriptures.* "Declared to be the Son
   of God, with power by the resurrection from the dead"
   (Romans 1:4). "God hath made this same Jesus, whom ye
   have crucified, both Lord and Christ" (Acts 2:36). "He
   will judge the world in righteousness by that man whom He
   hath ordained, whereof He hath given assurance unto all
   men, in that He hath raised Him from the dead" (Acts
   17:31).

2. *The claims of Christ.* Christ lived as we know and in the
   course of that life claimed to be the Son of God. He made
   such assertions as these —
   "I and the Father are one" (John 10:30). "I am the way,
   and the truth, and the life" (John 14:6). "He that believeth
   on Me shall never die" (John 11:25, 26). "The Son of
   Man must suffer many things — and the third day He shall
   rise again" (Luke 9:22). If He be risen from the dead
   then His loftiest claims are confirmed from the throne and
   we can see Him — the Son of God.

**B. With the Resurrection of Jesus Christ Stands or Falls
Christ's Whole Work for Our Redemption.**

1. *If Christ is not risen He died only as a martyr.* If He died,
   like other men — if that awful bony hand has got its grip
   upon Him too, then we have no proof that the cross was
   anything but a martyr's cross.

2. *If Christ is not risen there is no salvation.* His resurrection
   is the proof of His completed work of redemption. It is the
   proof that His death was the ransom for us. His resurrection is the condition of His present activity. If He has not

risen, He has not put away sin; and if He has not put it away by the sacrifice of Himself, none has, and it remains.

CONCLUSION

There is nothing between us and darkness, despair, death, but the ancient message, "I declare unto you the gospel which I preached, by which ye are saved if ye keep in memory what I preached unto you, how that Christ died for our sins according to the Scriptures, and that He was raised the third day according to the Scriptures" (I Corinthians 15:1-4).

21

Sons and Heirs

> *If children, then heirs, heirs of God and joint-heirs with Christ.* — Romans 8:17*

THERE is a sublime and wonderful mutual possession of which Scripture speaks much wherein the Lord is the inheritance of Israel, and Israel is the inheritance of the Lord. This being clearly understood at the outset, we shall be prepared to follow the Apostle's course of thought while he points out the conditions upon which the possession of that inheritance depends. It is children of God who are heirs of God.

I. NO INHERITANCE WITHOUT SONSHIP.

A. Natural Blessings Require a Natural Capacity to Receive Them.

1. *Only the eye perceives the light.* Always and necessarily the capacity or organ of reception precedes and determines the bestowment of blessings. The light falls everywhere, but only the eye drinks it in.

2. *Lower orders of creatures do not participate in the gifts belonging to higher forms of life.* Man has higher gifts simply because he has higher capacities. All creatures are plunged in the same boundless ocean of Divine beneficence and bestowment, and into each there flows just that, and no more, which each, by the make and constitution that God has given him, is capable of receiving.

B. Spiritual Blessings Require a Spiritual Capacity for Their Reception.

---

* From *Sermons Preached in Manchester*, First Series.

1. *Man must be adapted and prepared for the present blessings of salvation.* Inasmuch as God's deliverance is not a deliverance from a mere arbitrary and outward punishment: inasmuch as God's salvation, though it be deliverance from the penalty as well as from the guilt of sin, is by no means chiefly a deliverance from outward consequences, but a removal of the nature and disposition that makes these outward consequences certain, — therefore a man cannot be saved upon any other condition than this, that his soul shall be adapted and prepared for the reception and enjoyment of the blessing of a spiritual salvation.

2. *Man must be adapted and prepared for the future blessings of salvation.* There is no inheritance of heaven without sonship; because all the blessings of that future life are of a spiritual character. God is the heritage of His people.

II. NO SONSHIP WITHOUT A SPIRITUAL BIRTH.

A. Sonship Is Not Innate, but Men Become Sons of God After Birth by a Divine Act.

1. *The distinction between the general manifestation of God to all men and the specific relationship of God to some men by virtue of their faith.* John 1:9, 12. Whatever else may be taught in John's words, surely they do teach us this, that the sonship of which he speaks does not belong to man as man, is not a relation into which we are born by natural birth, that we become sons after we are men, that those who become sons are not co-extensive with those who are lighted by the Light, but consist of so many of that greater number as receive Him.

2. *The contrast between the sons of God and the world.* I John 3:10; John 8:42, 44. These are but specimens of a whole cycle of Scripture statements which in every form of necessary implication, and of direct statement, set forth the principle that he who is born again of the Spirit, and he only, is a son of God.

B. The Implications of Sonship.

1. *Communication of life.* It involves that the father and the child shall have kindred life — the Father bestowing and the child possessing a life which is derived; and because derived, kindred; and because kindred, unfolding itself in likeness to the Father that gave it.

2. *Reciprocity of love.* It requires that between the Father's heart and the child's heart there shall pass, in blessed interchange and quick correspondence, answering love, flashing backwards and forwards like the lightning that touches the earth and rises from it again.

III. NO SPIRITUAL BIRTH WITHOUT CHRIST.

A. Man Cannot Save Himself.

1. *Because the new life is in full accord with God.* It unfolds itself in certain holy character and affections and desires, the throbbing of the whole soul in full accord and harmony with the Divine character and will.

2. *Because man is sinful.* Man cannot make the new life for himself because of the habit of sin and because of the guilt and punishment of sin.

B. Christ Came to Save Men.

1. *The nature of the salvation He procured.* Christ came to make you and me live again as we never lived before — possessors of God's love, tenanted and used by the Divine Spirit, with affections we could not kindle, with purposes in our souls which we never could put there.

2. *The cost of the salvation He procured.* Christ has carried in the golden urn of His humanity a new spirit and a new life which He has set down in the midst of the race; and the urn was broken on the cross of Calvary, and the water flowed out, and whithersoever that water comes there is life and whithersoever it comes not there is death!

IV. NO CHRIST WITHOUT FAITH.

It is not enough, brethren, that we should go through all these steps, if we then go utterly astray at the end, by forgetting that there is only one way by which we become partakers of any of the benefits and blessings that Christ has wrought out. Unless we are wedded to Jesus Christ by the simple act of trust in His mercy and His power, Christ is nothing to us.

A. The Necessity of Faith.

1. *The benefits wrought by Christ are received only on the basis of faith.*

2. *Without faith Christ is nothing to us.*

B. The Meaning of Faith.

1. *It is trust.*

2. *It is rest.*

CONCLUSION

If you have not your foot upon the lowest round of the ladder (faith) you will never come within sight of the blessed face of Him who stands at the tip of it, and who looks down to you at this moment, saying to you, "My child, wilt thou not cry unto Me, 'Abba, Father'?"

22

Suffering with Christ, A Condition of Glory with Christ

> *Joint heirs with Christ, if so be that we suffer with Him, that we may be also glorified together.*
> — Romans 8:17*

IN THE former part of this verse the Apostle tells us that in order to be heirs of God we must become sons through and joint-heirs with Christ. The one, — being sons, "joint-heirs with Christ," is the root of the whole matter; the other, — "the suffering with Him," is but the various process by which from the root there come "the blade, and the ear, and the full corn in the ear." Given the sonship — if it is to be worked out into power and beauty, there must be the suffering with Christ. But unless there be sonship, there is no possibility of inheriting God; discipline and suffering will be of no use at all.

I. SONSHIP WITH CHRIST NECESSARILY INVOLVES SUFFERING WITH HIM.

A. The Believer's Fellowship in Christ's Sufferings.

The sufferings of Christ, both because of the nature which bore them, and of the aspect which they wore in regard to us are in their source, in their intensity, in their character, and consequences, unapproachable, incapable of repetition. But then, do not let us forget that the very books and writers in the New Testament that preach Christ's sole, all-sufficient, eternal redemption for the world by His sufferings and death, turn around and say to us, too, "Be planted together in the

---

* From *Sermons Preached in Manchester*, First Series.

likeness of His death"; "fill up that which is behind of the
sufferings of Christ."

1. *Christ's sufferings caused by His contact with the world.*

2. *Christ's sufferings caused by His temptations.* There was
no sin within Him, no tendency to sin, no yielding to the
evil that assailed. But yet, when that dark power stood
by His side and said, "If Thou be the Son of God, cast
Thyself down," it was a real temptation and not a sham
one.

3. *The death of Christ typical of the believer's daily dying.*
The death of Christ [in addition to its redemptive aspect
—Ed.] is a type of the Christian's life, which is to be one
long-protracted and daily dying to sin, to self, to the world.

B. The Companionship of Christ With the Suffering Believer.

1. *It is a consoling fact that Christ is with us in our afflictions.*
We need not hold that there is no reference here to that
comforting thought, "In all our affliction, He is afflicted."

2. *It is a consoling fact that Christ has trod the path of suffering before us.* Brethren, you and I have — each of us —
one in one way, and one in another, all in some way, all in
the right way, none in too severe a way, none in too slight
a way — to tread in the path of sorrow; and is it not a
blessed thing, as we go along through that dark valley of
the shadow of death down into which the sunniest paths
go sometimes, to come amidst the twilight and gathering
clouds, upon tokens that Jesus has been on the road before us?

3. *It is a consoling fact that no affliction is too small for Him
to bear with us.* Whether it be a poison from an serpent
sting, or whether it be poison from a million of buzzing tiny
mosquitoes; if there be a smart, go to Him and He will
help you bear it. He will do more, He will bear it with
you, for if so be that we suffer with Him, He suffers with
us, and our oneness with Christ brings about a community
of possessions whereby it becomes true of each trusting

soul in its relations to Him, that "all mine (joys and sorrows alike) are thine and all thine are mine."

II. THIS COMMUNITY OF SUFFERING IS A PREPARATION FOR THE COMMUNITY OF GLORY.

A. The Way a Man is Made Fit for Glory.

1. *It is not by discipline.* One thing at any rate is very certain,
   it is not the discipline that fits. That which fits goes before
   the discipline, and the discipline only develops the fitness.

2. *It is a past act.* "God *hath made* us meet for the inheritance
   of the saints in light," says the Apostle. This is a past act.

3. *It is when a man turns to Christ.* The preparedness for
   heaven comes at the moment — if it be a momentary
   act — when a man turns to Christ. "This day thou shalt be
   with Me in paradise" — fit for the inheritance.

B. The Development of Man's Fitness for Glory.

1. *Discipline develops man's fitness for heaven.* In His mercy
   He is leaving you here, training you, disciplining you,
   cleansing you, making you to be polished shafts in His
   quiver.

2. *Discipline is a seal of sonship.*

3. *Discipline prepares the believer for greater rewards in
   heaven.* And so learn to look upon all trial as being at once
   the seal of your sonship and the means by which God puts
   it within your power to win a higher place, a loftier throne,
   a nobler crown.

III. INHERITANCE IS THE NECESSARY RESULT OF SUFFERING.

A. The Ground of Possessing the Inheritance.

1. *It is not merely compensation.* It is not only because the joy
   hereafter seems required in order to vindicate God's love

to His children, who here reap sorrow from their sonship, that the discipline of life cannot but end in blessedness.

2. *It is union with Christ.* The suffering results from our union with Christ. That union must needs culminate in glory.

B. The Certainty of Possessing the Inheritance.

1. *Union with Christ.* But the inheritance is sure to all who here suffer with Christ, because the one cause — union with the Lord — produces both the present result of fellowship in His sorrows and the future result in His joy, of possession.

2. *Christ's present possession of the inheritance.*

3. *The design of trials to prepare us for heaven.* The inheritance is sure because earth's sorrows not merely require to be repaid by its peace, but because they have an evident design to fit us for it and it would be destructive to all faith in God's wisdom, and God's knowledge of His own purposes, not to believe that what He has wrought for us will be given to us.

CONCLUSION

Measure the greatness of the glory by what has preceded it. God takes all these years of life and all the sore trials and afflictions that belong inevitably to an earthly career and works them in, into the blessedness that shall come.

23

What Lasts

> *Whether there be prophecies, they shall fail; whether there be tongues, they shall cease; whether there be knowledge, it shall vanish away . . . And now abideth faith, hope, charity, these three . . .*
> —**I Corinthians 13:8, 13***

WE discern the Apostle's thought best by omitting the intervening verses and connecting these two. When we thus unite them there is disclosed the Apostle's intention of contrasting two sets of things, three in each. There also, comes out distinctly that the point mainly intended by the contrast is the transiency of the one and the permanence of the other.

I. THE THINGS THAT ARE TRANSIENT.

A. Present Modes of Apprehension.

1. *They shall cease because the imperfect shall be absorbed into the perfect.* "Knowledge, it shall cease," and as the Apostle goes on to explain, in the verses which I have passed over for my present purpose, it shall cease because the perfect will absorb into itself the imperfect, as the inrushing tide will obliterate the little pools in the rocks on the seashore.

2. *They shall cease because they are indirect and there it shall be immediate.* For another reason, the knowledge, the mode of apprehension belonging to the present will pass — because here it is indirect and there it will be immediate. "We shall know face to face," which is what philosophers call intuition.

---

* From *Triumphant Certainties.*

B. Present Modes of Utterance.

1. *There will be new methods of communication in heaven.* Modes of utterance will cease. With new experiences will come new methods of communication; as a man can speak and a beast can only growl or bark. So a man in heaven, with new experiences, will have new methods of communication.

2. *The comparison between the present mode of communication and that of the future.* The comparison between that mode of utterance which we now have and that which we shall then possess will be like the difference between the old-fashioned semaphore that used to wave about clumsy wooden arms in order to convey intelligence, and the telegraph.

II. THE THINGS THAT ARE PERMANENT.

A. Faith.

1. *Its relation to hope and love.* "So then, abideth these three, faith, hope, love." Paul takes these three nouns and couples them with a verb in the singular. Do not correct the grammar and spoil the sense, but discern what he means, that the two latter come out of the former and that without it they are nought and that it without them is dead.

2. *Its essence.* The essence of faith is not the absence of the person trusted, but the emotion of trust which goes out to the person, present or absent. In its deepest meaning of absolute dependence and happy confidence, faith abides through all the glories and the lustres of the heavens.

B. Hope.

1. *The difference between earthly and Christian hope.* Our hopes, apart from the revelation of God in Jesus Christ, are but the balancings of probabilities and the scale is often dragged down by the clutch of eager desires. Only the Christian has a rock foundation on which he can build his hope.

2. *The reason hope abides.* The future presents itself to us as the continual communication of an inexhaustible God to our

progressively capacious and capable spirits. In that continual communication there is continual progress. Wherever there is progress there must be hope.

C. Love.

1. *The abiding nature of love.* I need not, I suppose, enlarge upon that thought which nobody denies, that love is the eternal form of the human relation to God. It, too, like the mercy which it clasps, "endureth forever."

2. *The reason love is greatest.* It is greater than its linked sisters, because whilst faith and hope belong only to a creature and are dependent and expectant of some good to come to themselves and correspond to something which is in God in Christ, the love which springs from faith and hope not only corresponds to, but resembles that from which it comes and by which it lives. The love that is in man is like the love that is in God.

III. THE THINGS THAT FOLLOW FROM ALL THIS.

A. The True Understanding of Abiding Love.

1. *A false notion of love.* I do not use the word charity. Charity has come to mean an indulgent estimate of other people's faults or the giving of money to other people's necessities. These are what the people who do not care much about Paul's theology generally suppose that he means here. But these do not exhaust his meaning.

2. *The true idea of love.* Paul's notion of love is the response of the human love to the Divine, which Divine is received into the heart by faith in Jesus Christ. And his notion of love which never fails is love to men, which is but one stream of the great river of love to God.

B. The Highest Conception of the Christian's Future Condition.

1. *A danger to be avoided.* It is very easy to bewilder ourselves with speculations and theories of another life. It is easy to let ourselves be led away by turning rhetoric into

revelation and accepting the symbols of the New Testament as if they carried anything more than images of the realities.

2. *The essence of life in heaven.* The elements of the imperfect, Christlike life of earth are the essence of the perfect, Godlike life in heaven. "Now abide these three, faith, hope, love."

C. The Christian's Life Should Be Shaped in Accordance With These Certainties.

1. *The relation of the transient and the permanent in the Christian's life.* The dropping away of the transient things is no argument for neglecting or despising them; for our handling of them makes our characters and our characters abide. But it is an excellent argument to use the transient as that it shall help us towards that which does not pass.

2. *The importance of preparing for the future.* Suppose you knew that you were to go somewhere and you never did a single thing towards getting ready or preparing yourself. Would you be a wise man? But that is what a great many are doing.

CONCLUSION

Cultivate the high things, the permanent things; then death will not wrench you violently from all that you have been and cared for; but it will usher you into the perfect form of all that you have been and done upon earth.

24

Transformation By Beholding

We all with open face beholding as in a glass the glory of the Lord, are changed into the same image.

— II Corinthians 3:18*

JUDAISM had the one lawgiver who beheld God, while the people tarried below. Christianity leads us all to the mount of vision. Moses veiled the face that shone with the irradiation of Deity. We with unveiled faces are to shine among men. He had a momentary gleam; we have a perpetual light. Moses' face shone, but the luster was but skin deep. But the light that we have is inward and works transformation into its own likeness.

I. THE CHRISTIAN LIFE IS A LIFE OF CONTEMPLATING AND REFLECTING CHRIST.

A. The Meaning of "Beholding in a Glass."

1. *The requirement of the context.* It is a question whether the single word rendered "beholding as in a glass" means that, or "reflecting as a glass does." The latter seems more in accordance with the requirements of the context and with the truth of the matter in hand. On the whole, it seems better to suppose that Paul meant "mirroring," than "seeing in a mirror."

2. *The actual force of the expression.* But, whatever the exact force of the word, the thing intended includes both acts. There is no reflection of the light without a previous reception of the light.

---

* From *Sermons Preached in Manchester,* Second Series.

3. *The truth presented.* Thus, then, we may say that we have in our text the Christian life described as one of contemplation and manifestation of the light of God.

B. The Object of the Vision.

1. *It is Jesus Christ.*

2. *It is the glory of Jesus Christ.* The glory which we behold and give back is not the incomprehensible, incommunicable luster of the absolute Divine perfectness, but the glory which was manifested in loving, pitying words, and loveliness of perfect deeds; the glory of the will resigned to God, and of God dwelling in and working through the will; the glory of faultless and complete manhood, and therein of the express image of God.

C. The Nature of the Vision.

1. *It is a spiritual perception.* That seeing which is affirmed to be possible and actually bestowed in Christ, is the beholding of him with the soul by faith; the immediate direct consciousness of His presence, the perception of Him in His truth by the mind, the sense of Him in His love by the heart, the contact with His gracious energy in our recipient and opening spirits.

2. *It is a perception that all believers may have.* "We, all." This vision does not belong to any select handful. Christ reveals Himself to all His servants in the measure of their desire after Him.

3. *It is a contemplation involving reflection.* What we *see* we shall certainly *show.* Nor is it only that our fellowship with Christ will, as a matter of course, show itself in our characters and beauty born of that communion "shall pass into our face," but we are also called on, as Paul puts it here, to make direct conscious efforts for the communication of the light which we behold.

II. THE LIFE OF CONTEMPLATION IS A LIFE OF GRADUAL TRANSFORMATION.

A. The Contrast Between the Brightness on Moses' Face and the Glory Which the Christian Beholds.

1. *The brightness on Moses' face lacked permanence and transforming power, thereby illustrating the powerlessness of the law to change the moral character.*

2. *The glory of the Lord which the Christian beholds has permanence and transforming power, proclaiming Christian progress and assimilation to Christ.*

B. The Work of Contemplation.

1. *The prerequisite to contemplation:* Christ in us. The light must first sink in before it can shine out. In deep inward beholding we must have Christ in our hearts, that He may shine forth from our lives.

2. *The nature of contemplation:* gaze of love and trust. It is not the mere beholding, but the gaze of love and trust that moulds us by silent sympathy into the likeness of His wondrous beauty, who is fairer than the children of men.

3. *The practical result of contemplation:* Christ-likeness. Spirits that dwell with Christ become Christ-like. Such transformation, it must be remembered, comes gradually. The language of the text regards it as a life-long process.

III. THE LIFE OF CONTEMPLATION FINALLY BECOMES A LIFE OF COMPLETE ASSIMILATION.

A. Transformation Issues Into Complete Assimilation.

1. *It is completed in heaven in corporeal likeness.* We look for the merciful exercise of His mighty working to "change the body of our lowliness, that it may be fashioned like unto the body of His glory" (Philippians 3:21); and that physical change in the resurrection of the just rightly bulks very large in good men's expectations.

2. *It begins on earth in spiritual likeness.* The glorious, corporeal life like our Lord's, which is promised for heaven,
is great and wonderful, but it is only the issue and last
result of the far greater change in the spiritual nature which
by faith and love begins here. His true image is that we
should feel as He does, should think as He does, should
will as He does; have the same sympathies, the same loves,
the same attitude towards God and the same attitudes
towards men.

B. **The Significance of the Term "Same Image."**

1. *The image we behold.*

2. *The likeness of all who become like him.* As if he had said,
"Various as we are in disposition and character, unlike in
the history of our lives, and all the influences these have
had upon us, differing in everything but the common relation to Jesus Christ, we are all growing like the same image
and we shall come to be perfectly like it and yet each retain
his own distinct individuality."

3. *The aggregate perfectness of the individual church.* In the
Epistle to the Ephesians Paul says that the Christian ministry is to continue till a certain point of progress has been
reached which he describes as our *all* coming to a "perfect
man" (Ephesians 4:13). The whole of us together make a
perfect man: the whole make one image.

CONCLUSION

The law of the transformation is the same for earth and for
heaven. Here we see Him in part and beholding we grow like
Him. There we shall see Him as He is and the likeness will be
complete.

25

Measureless Power and Endless Glory

> *Now unto Him that is able to do exceeding abundantly above all that we ask or think, according to the power that worketh in us, unto Him be glory in the Church by Christ Jesus throughout all ages, world without end. Amen.*
>
> — Ephesians 3:20-21*

THE form of our text marks the confidence of Paul's prayer. The exuberant fervor of his faith, as well as the natural impetuosity and ardor, comes out in the heaped-up words expressive of immensity and duration. He is gazing on God confident that he has not asked in vain.

I. THE MEASURE OF THE POWER.

A. According to the Riches of His Glory (3:16).

1. *Its explanation.* The "riches of His glory" can be nothing less than the whole uncounted abundance of that majestic and far-shining Nature, as it pours itself forth in the dazzling perfectness of its own self-manifestation.

2. *Its effect.* Absolute perfectness, the full transmutation of our dark, cold being into the reflected image of His own burning brightness, the ceaseless replenishing of our own spirits with all graces and gladness akin to His, the eternal growth of the soul upward and Godward.

B. According to His Mighty Power, which He Wrought in Christ When He Raised Him from the Dead (1:19-20).

---

*From *The Secret of Power.*

108

1. *Its purport.* The Lord, in the glory of His risen life, and in the riches of the gifts which He received when He ascended up on high, is the pattern for us and the power which fulfils its own pattern.

2. *Its purpose.* The limits of that power will not be reached until every Christian soul is perfectly assimilated to that likeness nor till every Christian soul is raised to participation in Christ's dignity and sits on His throne.

C. According to the Power Which Works in Us (3:20).

1. *Its meaning.* What power is that but the power of the Spirit of God?

2. *Its outcome.* The effects already produced and the experiences we have already had carry in them the pledge of completeness.

II. THE RELATION OF THE DIVINE WORKING TO OUR THOUGHTS AND DESIRES.

A. The Extent of the Divine Working.

1. *It is "beyond all things."* What he means by this is more fully expressed in the words: "exceeding abundantly above what we ask or think."

2. *It refers especially to spiritual blessings.* The rapturous words of our text are only true in a very modified and partial sense about God's working for us in the world. It is His work in us concerning which they are absolutely true.

B. The Wonder of the Divine Working.

1. *It is the power of the Triune God.* As regards the working of God on our spiritual lives, this passing beyond the bounds of thought and desire is but the necessary result of the fact that the only measure of the power is God Himself in that threefold being.

2. *It is more than we realize and receive.* In every act of His quickening grace, in every God-given increase of our knowledge of God, in every bestowment of His fulness, there is

always more bestowed than we receive, more than we know even while we possess it.

C. The Reminders Concerning the Divine Working.

1. *While the Divine working exceeds our thoughts and prayers, it is meant to draw them after it.* While our thoughts and prayers can never react to the full perception or reception of the gift, the exuberant amplitude with which it reaches far beyond both is meant to draw both after it.

2. *Our thoughts and desires determine the amount of grace received.* The grace which we receive has no limit or measure but the fulness of God, the working limit, which determines what we receive of the grace, is those very thoughts and wishes which it surpasses. We may have as much of God as we can hold, or as much as we wish.

III. THE GLORY WHICH SPRINGS FROM THE DIVINE WORK.

A. The Doxology.

1. *It is both a prophecy and a prayer.* This doxology is at once a prophecy that the working of God's power on His redeemed children will issue in setting forth the radiance of His name yet more, and a prayer that it may.

2. *The highest exhibition of God's character for reverence and love is in His work on Christian souls and the effect produced.* He reckons it His highest praise that He has redeemed men, and by His indwelling them, fills them with His own fulness.

B. The Offerers of the Glory.

1. *The persons.* The chiefest praise and brightest glory accrues to Him "in the Church in Christ Jesus."[1] His glory is to shine in the Church, the theatre of His power, the standing demonstration of the might of His redeeming love.

---

1. The best texts read: "in the church and in Christ Jesus," meaning that God is glorified both in the church and in Christ.—Ed.

2. *The prerequisite.* His glory is to be set forth by men on condition that they are "in Christ," living and moving in Him, in that mysterious but most real union.

IV. THE ETERNITY OF THE WORK AND OF THE PRAISE.

A. The Scriptural Statement.

1. *The Authorized Version:* "throughout all ages world without end."

2. *The literal rendering:* "to all generations of the age of the ages."

B. The Meaning of the Scriptural Statement.

1. *"To all generations":* expressive of duration as long as birth and death shall last.

2. *"The age of the ages":* pointing to that endless epoch whose moments are ages.

3. *The blending of the two expressions:* an unconscious acknowledgement that the speech of earth, saturated with the coloring of time, breaks down in the attempt to express the thought of eternity.

C. The Compass of the Statement.

The work is to go on forever and ever and with it the praise. As the ages which are the beats of the pendulum of eternity come and go, more and more of God's power will flow out to us and more and more of God's glory will be manifested in us.

1. *Work.*

2. *Praise.*

CONCLUSION

Let His grace work in you, and yield yourselves to Him, that His fulness may fill your emptiness.

26

The Race and the Goal

This one thing I do, forgetting those things which are behind, and reaching forth unto those things which are before, I press toward the mark for the prize.
— Philippians 3:13, 14*

THE Apostle here is letting us see the secret of his own life and telling us what made him the sort of Christian that he was. He counsels wise obliviousness, wise anticipation, strenuous concentration; and these are the things that contribute to success in any field of life.

I. MAKE GOD'S AIM YOUR AIM.

A. The Example of Paul.

1. *The testimony of the immediate context.* He regards the aim towards which he strains as being the aim which Christ had in view in his conversion (Verses 12, 13b).

2. *The summary of the teaching of the immediate context.* He took God's purpose in calling and Christ's purpose in redeeming him as being his great object in life. God's aim and Paul's were identical.

B. God's Aim.

1. *The aim stated.* What, then, is the aim of God in all that He has done for us? The production in us of God-like and God-pleasing character.

2. *The importance of the aim.* For this all the discipline of life is set in motion. For this we were created; for this we have

* From *The Wearied Christ.*

been redeemed. For this Jesus Christ lived and suffered and died. For this God's Spirit is poured out upon the world.

C. The Results of the Acceptance of God's Aim.

1. *It changes man's estimate of the meaning and true nature of events.* It will give nobleness and blessedness to our lives. How different all our estimates of the meaning and true nature of events would be, if we kept before us that their intention was to mold us to the likeness of our Lord and Savior!

2. *It changes a man's estimate of nearer objects and aims.* Men take these great powers which God has given them and use them to make money, to cultivate their intellects, to secure the gratification of earthly desires, to make a home for themselves; and all the while the great aim which ought to stand out clear and supreme is forgotten.

II. CONCENTRATE ALL EFFORT ON THIS ONE AIM.

A. The Aim is Consistent With All Occupations, Except Sin. It needs not that we should seek any remote or cloistered form of life, nor shear off any legitimate and common interests, but in them all we may be seeking for the one thing, the moulding of our characters into the shapes that are pleasing to Him.

B. The Requirements in Order to Keep This Aim Clear.

1. *To keep close to God.*

2. *To be surrendered to God.* To keep the aim clear is possible if we will do two things, keep ourselves close to God and be prepared to surrender much, laying our own wills, our own fancies, purposes, eager hopes and plans in His hands, and asking Him to help us that we may never lose sight of the only end which is an end in itself.

3. *To concentrate on the aim.* The conquering word is, "This one thing I do." If you want to be a Christian after God's pattern you have to make it your business to give the same

attention, the same concentration, the same unwavering energy to it which you do to your trade.

III. PURSUE THIS END WITH A WISE FORGETFULNESS.

A. The Meaning of "Forgetting the Things That Are Behind."

1. *The meaning stated negatively.* He does not mean that we are to cultivate obliviousness as to let God's mercies to us "lie, forgotten in unthankfulness, or without praises to die." Nor does he mean to tell us that we are to deny ourselves the solace of remembering the mercies which may, perhaps, have gone from us.

2. *The meaning stated positively.* He means that we should so forget as, by the oblivion, to strengthen our concentration.

B. The Application of "Forgetting the Things That Are Behind."

1. *Remember and forget past failures and faults.* Let us remember them in order that the remembrance may cultivate in us a wise chastening of our self-confidence. Let us forget our failures in so far as these might paralyze our hopes or make us fancy that future success is impossible where past failures frown.

2. *Remember and forget past successes and achievements.* Remember them for thankfulness, for hope, for counsel and instruction, but forget them when they tend to make us fancy that little more remains to be done; and forget them when they tend to make us think that such and such things are our line and of other virtues and graces and achievements of culture and of character, that these are not our line and not to be won by us.

IV. PURSUE THE AIM WITH A WISE, EAGER REACHING FORWARD.

A. The Expressiveness of "Reaching Forth."

1. *The English translation only partially expresses the meaning.* The Apostle employs a graphic word here, which is only partially expressed by that "reaching forth."

2. *The picture presented by the word.* "Reaching out over" is the full though clumsy rendering of the word; and it gives us the picture of a runner with his whole body thrown forward, his hand extended and his eye reaching even further than his hand, in eager anticipation of the mark and the prize.

B. **The Incentive of the Unattained.** The idealists see the unattained burning so clearly before them that all the unattained seems as nothing in their eyes. So life is saved from commonplace, is happily strung into fresh effort, is redeemed from flagging, monotony, and weariness.

1. *It gives an element of nobility to the lives of idealists.*

2. *It saves life from the common-place.*

C. **The Measure of Attainment May be Estimated by the Extent to Which the Unattained Is Clear to Us.**

1. *The blessing of having a boundless future.* They who have a boundless future before them have an endless source of inspiration, of energy, of buoyancy granted to them.

2. *The Christian has the greatest vision of a boundless future.* No man has such an absolutely boundless vision of the future as we have if we are Christian people. Only we can look thus forward.

CONCLUSION

Make God's aim your aim; concentrate your life's efforts upon it; pursue it with a wise forgetfulness; pursue it with an eager confidence of anticipation that shall not be put to shame.

27

Everlasting Consolation and Good Hope

> *Now our Lord Jesus Christ Himself, and God, even our Father, which hath loved us, and hath given us everlasting consolation and good hope through grace, comfort your hearts, and establish you in every good word and work.*
>
> — II Thessalonians 2:16, 17*

THIS is the second of the four brief prayers in this letter. We do not know the special circumstances under which these were written, but there are many allusions, both in the first and second epistles, which seem to indicate that they specially needed the gift of consolation.

I. THE DIVINE HEARERS OF THE PRAYER.

A. The Recognition of the Deity of Jesus Christ Was a Familiar Truth to the Thessalonian Christians.

1. *The accumulation of His august titles.* The first striking thing about this prayer is its emphatic recognition of the deity of Jesus Christ as a truth familiar to these Thessalonian converts. Note the solemn accumulation of His august titles, "Our Lord Jesus Christ Himself."

2. *The association of His name with the Father's.*

3. *The order of the names.* Note, the most remarkable order in which these two names occur — Jesus first, God second. The reason for the order may be found partly in the context

---

* From *Paul's Prayers.*

which has been naming Christ, but still more in the fact that whilst he writes, the Apostle is realizing the mediation of Christ and that the order of mention is the order of our approach. The Father comes to us in the Son; we come to the Father by the Son.

B. The Distinct Address to Christ as the Hearer of Prayer.

1. *The grammatical peculiarity.* The words which follow, that is, "comfort" and "stablish," are in the singular, whilst these two mighty and august names are their nominatives and would therefore, by all regularity, require a plural to follow them.

2. *The truth expressed by this grammatical peculiarity.* The phraseology is the expression of the great truth, "Whatsoever things the Father doeth, these also doth the Son likewise." And from it there gleam out unmistakably the great principles of the unity of action and the distinction of person between Father and Son in the depths of that infinite and mysterious Godhead.

3. *The testimony of this grammatical peculiarity.* Now all this is made the more remarkable and the stronger as a witness of the truth from the fact that it occurs in this incidental fashion and without a word of explanation or apology, as taking for granted that there was a background of teaching in the Thessalonian Church which had prepared the way for it and rendered it intelligible, as well as a background of conviction which had previously accepted it.

II. THE GREAT FACT ON WHICH THIS PRAYER BUILDS ITSELF.

A. The Implication of a Definite Historical Act.

1. *The statement of the implication.* The form of words in the original, "loved" and "given," all but necessarily requires us to suppose that their reference is to some one definite historical act in which the love was manifested, and, as love always does, found voice in giving.

2. *The act implied.* The gift of Jesus Christ is that in which everlasting consolation and good hope are bestowed upon

men. When our desires are widened out to the widest they must be based upon the great sacrifice of Jesus Christ.

B. The Gifts Bestowed.

1. *Everlasting comfort.* There is one source of comfort which, because it comes from an unchangeable Christ and communicates unfailing gifts of patience and insight and because it leads to everlasting blessedness and recompenses may well be called "eternal consolation."

2. *Good hope.* In the cross and in the Christ lie the foundation and the object of a hope which stands unique in excellence and sufficient in its firmness. "A good hope"; good because well founded; good because grasping worthy objects.

C. The Presupposition of Heaven's Logic.

1. *The statement of heaven's logic.* God has given; therefore God will give.

2. *Three suppositions.* It presupposes inexhaustible resources, unchangeable purposes of kindness, patience that is not disgusted and cannot be turned away by sin.

III. THE SPECIFICATION OF THE DESIRES INCLUDED IN THE PRAYER.

A. A Comforted Heart.

1. *The connection between the past gift of everlasting consolation and the present and future comfort of hearts.* God has bestowed the materials for comfort; God will give the comfort for which He has supplied the materials.

2. *Man's need met.* It is not enough for us that there should be calmness and consolation twining round the cross if we choose to pluck the fruit. We need and we have an indwelling God who, by that Spirit who is the Comforter, will make for each of us the everlasting consolation our individual possession.

B. A Stable Heart.

1. *Man's natural instability.* We all know how vacillating, how driven to and fro by gusts of passion and winds of doctrine and forces of earth our resolutions and spirits are.

2. *The secret of stability.* If we have Christ in our hearts He will be our consolation first and our stability next. Our hearts may be like some land-locked lake that knows no tide. "His heart is fixed, trusting in the Lord."

C. A Fruitful Heart.

1. *A man's life can be characterized by practical righteousness.* There is no reason why each of us should not appropriate and make our own the forms of goodness to which we are least naturally inclined and cultivate and possess a symmetrical, fully-developed, all-round goodness in some humble measure after the pattern of Jesus Christ our Lord.

2. *The source of practical righteousness.* Practical righteousness, "in every good word and work," is the outcome of all the sacred and secret consolations and blessings that Jesus Christ imparts. We get our goodness where we get our consolation, from Jesus Christ and His Cross.

CONCLUSION

All your hopes will be like a child's castles on the sand unless your hope is fixed on Him. You may have everlasting consolation, you may have a hope which will enable you to look severely on the ills of life. You may have a calm and steadied heart. You may have an all-round, stable, comprehensive goodness. But there is only one way to get these blessings and that is to grasp and make our own by simple faith that great gift, Jesus Christ.

28

The Gospel of the Glory of the Happy God

The glorious gospel of the blessed God.
— I Timothy 1:11*

TWO remarks will prepare the way for our consideration of this text. The first is that the proper rendering is given in the Revised Version — "The gospel of the glory," not "The glorious gospel." The Apostle is not telling us what kind of thing the gospel is, but what it is about. Then the other remark is with reference to the meaning of the word "blessed." The word which is used here describes Him altogether apart from what man says of Him, as what He is in Himself, the "blessed," or, as we might almost say, the "happy God."

I. THE REVELATION OF GOD IN JESUS CHRIST IS THE GLORY OF GOD.

A. The Significance of the Words "Glory of God."

1. *The Old Testament meaning of "the glory."* Now what do we mean by "the glory"? I think, perhaps, that the question may be most simply answered by remembering the definite meaning of the word in the Old Testament. There it designates usually, that the supernatural and lustrous light which dwelt between the cherubim, the symbol of the presence and of the self-manifestation of God.

2. *The explanation of the phrase "the glory of God."* The glory of God is the sum-total of the light that streams from His self-revelation, considered as being the object of adora-

---

* From *Christ in the Heart.*

120

tion and praise by a world that gazes upon Him. The Apostle, just because to him the Gospel was the story of the Christ who lived and died, declares that in this story of a human life, patient, meek, limited, despised, rejected, and at last crucified, lies, brighter than all other flashings of the Divine light, the very heart of the luster and palpitating center and frontal source of all the radiance with which God has flooded the world. The history of Jesus Christ is the glory of God.

B. Three Considerations Concerning the Substance of the Gospel.

1. *Christ is the self-revelation of God.* What force of logic is there in the Apostle's words: "God commendeth His love toward us in that whilst we were yet sinners Christ died for us," unless there is some altogether different connection between the God who commends His love and the Christ who dies to commend it, than exists between a mere man and God. In that man Christ Jesus "we behold His glory, the glory of the only begotten of the Father." We see in Him the manifest Deity. Listen to that voice, "He that hath seen Me hath seen the Father," and bow before the story of the human life of Jesus Christ as being the revelation of the indwelling God.

2. *The Divine self-communication in Christ.* In that wondrous story of the life and death of our Lord Jesus Christ the high-water mark of Divine self-communication has been touched and reached. All the energies of the Divine nature are embodied there. The "riches both of the wisdom of the knowledge of God" are in the cross and passion of our Savior. The whole Godhead, so to speak, flows from the cross of Christ into the hearts of men.

3. *The center of the glory of God is the love of God.* The text implies still further that the true living, flashing center of the glory of God is the love of God. If we rightly understand the text, then we learn this, that the true heart of the glory is tenderness and love. The gospel is the Gospel of the glory of God because it is all summed up in the one

word — "God so loved the world that He gave His only begotten Son."

II. THE REVELATION OF GOD IN JESUS CHRIST IS THE BLESSEDNESS OF GOD.

A. **The Fact of the Blessedness of God.** The Bible's God "delighteth in mercy," rejoiceth in His gifts and is glad when men accept them. If we went no further, to me there is infinite beauty and mighty consolation and strength in that one thought — the happy God. The Psalmist saw deeply into the Divine nature when he exclaimed, "Thou makest us to drink of the rivers of Thy pleasures."

B. **The Source of the Blessedness of God.** The context seems to suggest that howsoever the Divine nature must be supposed to be blessed in its own absolute and boundless perfectness, an element in the blessedness of God Himself arises from His self-communication through the Gospel to the world. The blessed God is blessed because He is God. But He is blessed too because He is loving and therefore the giving God.

1. *God's own perfectness.*

2. *God's self-communication through the Gospel to men.*

III. THE REVELATION OF GOD IN JESUS CHRIST IS GOOD NEWS TO ALL.

A. **The Loss of the Significance of the Gospel.** How the word "gospel" has become tarnished and enfeebled by constant use and unreflective use, so that it slips glibly off my tongue and falls without producing any effect upon your hearts. It needs to be freshened up by considering what it really means.

1. *By constant usage.*

2. *By thoughtless usage.*

B. **The True Meaning of the Gospel.** Here are, we like men shut up in a beleagured city, hopeless, helpless, with no power to break out or to raise the seige; provisions failing, death certain. And the message is this: — God is love; and that you may know that He is, He has sent you His Son who died on the cross, the sacrifice for a world's sin.

1. *The deliverance of captives.*

2. *The deliverance of captives on the ground of Christ's death.*

CONCLUSION

Let me beseech you, welcome the message; do not turn away from the Word from heaven which will bring life and blessedness to all your hearts! Some of you have turned away long enough, some of you, perhaps, are fighting with the temptation to do so again even now. Let me press that ancient Gospel upon your acceptance, that Christ the Son of God has died for you, and lives to bless and help you. So shall you find that "as cold water to a thirsty soul, so is this best of all news from the far country."

29

A Prisoner's Dying Thoughts

> *I am now ready to be offered, and the time of my departure is at hand. I have fought a good fight, I have finished my course, I have kept the faith: henceforth there is laid up for me a crown of righteousness.*
> — II Timothy 4:6-8*

THESE familiar words of our text bring us a very sweet and wonderful picture of the prisoner, so near his end. How beautifully they show his calm waiting for the last hour and the bright forms which lightened for him the darkness of the cell. These words refer to the past, the present, the future. "I have fought — the time of my departure is come — henceforth there is laid up."

I. THE QUIET COURAGE WHICH LOOKS DEATH IN THE FACE WITHOUT A TREMOR.

A. **The Tone of the Language of the Text.** As the revised version more accurately gives it, "I am already being offered" — the process is begun, the initial steps of his sacrifice — "and the time of my departure is come." There is no sign of excitement, no tremor of emotion, no affectation of stoicism in the simple sentences.

B. **The Occasion of the Text.** He is led to speak about himself only in order to enforce his exhortation to Timothy to put his shoulder to the wheel and do his work for Christ with all his might.

---

* From *The Secret of Power.*

C. The Subject of the Text.

1. *Its effect on Paul.* The anticipation of death did not dull his interest in God's work in the world as witness the warnings and exhortations of the context. It did not withdraw his sympathies from his companions. It did not hinder him from pursuing his studies and pursuits, nor for providing for small matters of daily convenience. (II Timothy 4: 9-22).

2. *Its manner of expression.* (a) Offering or more particularly a drink offering or libation, "I am already being poured out." No doubt the special reason for the selection of this figure is Paul's anticipation of a violent death. (b) Departure. Death is a going away, or, as Peter calls it an exodus.

II. THE PEACEFUL LOOK BACKWARDS.

A. The Pauline Estimate of Life.

1. *A contest which requires struggle.* The world, both of men and things, has had to be grappled with and mastered. His own sinful nature has had to be kept under by sheer force and every moment has been resistance to subtle omnipresent forces that have sought to thwart his aspirations and hamper his performances.

2. *A race which requires effort.* This speaks of continuous advance in one direction, and more emphatically still, of effort that sets the lungs panting and strains every muscle to the utmost.

3. *A stewardship which requires fidelity.* He has kept the faith as a sacred deposit committed to him, of which he has been a good steward and which he is now ready to return to the Lord.

B. The Results of the Pauline Estimate of Life.
Such a view of life makes it radiant and fair while it lasts and makes the heart calm when the hour comes to leave it all behind. So thinking of the past there may be a sense of not unwelcome lightening from a load of responsibility when we have all the stress and strain of the conflict behind us.

1. *While life lasts it is radiant and fair.*

2. *When death approaches it makes the heart calm.*

C. **The Requirement of the Pauline Estimate of Life.** Such an estimate has nothing in common with self-complacency. It coexists with a profound consciousness of many a sin, many a defeat, and much unfaithfulness. It belongs only to a man who, conscious of these, is "looking for the mercy of the Lord Jesus Christ unto eternal life" (Jude 21), and is the direct result of lowly self-abasement, and contrite faith in Him.

1. *Absence of self-complacency.*

2. *Dependence upon God's mercy.*

3. *Self-abasement.*

4. *Contrite faith in God.*

III. THE TRIUMPHANT LOOK FORWARD.

A. **The Reward.** In harmony with the images of the conflict and the race, the crown here is not the emblem of sovereignty, but of victory. The reward then which is meant by the emblem comes through effort and conflict. "A man is not crowned, except he strive" (II Timothy 2:5).

1. *It is not a sovereign's diadem.*

2. *It is the victor's wreath.*

B. **The Persons Rewarded.**

1. *The meaning of "crown of righteousness."* Righteousness alone can receive the reward. It is not the struggle or the conflict which wins it, not the works of strenuous service, but the moral nature expressed in these. It is, then, the crown of righteousness, as belonging by its very nature to such characters alone.

2. *The gift of righteousness.* The righteousness which clothes us in fair raiment and has a natural right to the wreath of victory is a gift as truly as the crown itself and is given to us all on the condition of our simple trust in Jesus Christ.

C. The Time of Rewarding. The crown is given at a time called by Paul "at that day," which is not the near day of his martyrdom, but that of his Lord's appearing. He does not speak of the fulness of the reward as being ready for him at death, but as being "henceforth laid up in heaven." So he looks forward beyond the grave.

1. *It is in "that day."*

2. *It is at the appearing of Jesus Christ.*

CONCLUSION

If we can humbly say, "To me to live is Christ," then it is well. Living by Him we may fight and conquer, may win and obtain. Living by Him, we may be ready quietly to lie down when the time comes and may have all the future filled with the blaze of a great hope, that grows brighter as the darkness thickens.

30

A Father's Discipline

*For they verily for a few days chastened
us after their own pleasure; but He for our
profit, that we might be partakers of His
holiness.* — Hebrews 12:10*

FEW words of Scripture have been oftener than
these laid as a healing balm on wounded hearts. They may
be long unnoticed on the page, like a lighthouse in calm sunshine, but sooner or later the stormy night falls and then
the bright beam flashes out and is welcome. They go very
deep into the meaning of life as a discipline; they tell us
how much better God's discipline is than that of the most
loving and wise of parents and they give that superiority as
a reason for our yielding more entire and cheerful obedience
to Him than we do to such.

I. LIFE IS ONLY INTELLIGIBLE WHEN IT IS REGARDED AS EDUCATION OR DISCIPLINE.

A. **All Which Befalls Us Has a Will Behind it and Operates
Together to an End.** Life is not a heap of unconnected
incidents, like a number of links flung down on the ground, but
the links are a chain and the chain has a staple.

B. **Throughout Our Earthly Life We Are in a State of Pupil-
age.** Life is given to us to teach us how to live, to exercise our powers, to give us habits and facilities of working.
There is no meaning worthy of us — to say nothing of God —
in anything that we do, unless it is looked upon as schooling.

---

* From *The Victor's Crown.*

C. The Whole of This Life is an Education Towards Another. If this life is education, as is obvious upon its very face, then there is a place where we shall exercise the facilities that we have acquired here and manifest in loftier forms the characters which we here have made our own.

III. THE GUIDING PRINCIPLE OF THAT DISCIPLINE.

A. The Contrast Between the Principles of Human and Divine Discipline.

1. *Guiding principle of human discipline is the parents' conception of what is good for the child.* "They . . . as seemed good to them." Even in the most wise and unselfish training by an earthly parent there will mingle subjective elements, peculiarities of view and thought, and sometimes of passion and whim and other ingredients, which detract from the value of all such training.

2. *The guiding principle of Divine discipline is that which is profitable for us.* "He for our profit" — with no sidelong look to anything else and with an entirely wise knowledge of what is best for us, so that the result will be always and only for our good.

B. Truths Suggested by the Guiding Principle of Divine Discipline. There is no such thing as evil except the evil of sin. All that comes is good — of various sorts and various complexions, but all generically the same: The inundation comes up over the fields and men are in despair. It goes down and there is better soil for the fertilizing of our fields. All that men call evil in the material world has in it a soul of good.

1. *There is no such thing as evil except evil of sin.*

2. *All that comes is for our good.*

C. The Reality of Pain and Sorrow.

1. *It is right that we yield to the impressions made upon us by calamities.* The mission of our troubles would not be effected unless they did trouble us. The good that we get from a sorrow would not be realized unless we did sorrow. "Weep

for yourselves," said the Master, "and for your children" (Luke 23:28).

2. *It is wrong, to lose sight of the fact that the calamities are for our good.* God sends us many love-tokens, and amongst them are the great and the little annoyances and pains that beset our lives and on each of them, if we would look, we should see written, in His own hand, this inscription: "For your good."

III. THE GREAT AIM OF ALL THE DISCIPLINE.

A. The Greatness of the Aim. God trains us for an eternal end: "that we should be partakers of His holiness." The one object which is congruous with a man's nature and is stamped on his whole being as its only adequate end is that he should be like God. I may have made myself rich, cultured, learned, famous, refined, prosperous; but if I have not at least begun to be like God in purity, in will, in heart, then my whole career has missed the purpose for which I was made and for which all the discipline of life has been lavished upon me.

B. The Means of Reaching the Aim. That great and only worthy end may be reached by the ministration of circumstances and the discipline through which God passes us. These are not the only ways by which He makes us partakers of His holiness. There is the work of that Divine Spirit who is granted to every believer to breathe into him the holy breath of an immortal and incorruptible life. To work along with these is the influence that is brought to bear upon us by the circumstances in which we are placed and duties which we have to perform.

1. *The ministration of circumstances.*

2. *The ministration of discipline.*

3. *The ministration of the Holy Spirit.*

C. The Intention of Discipline.

1. *The statement* — They will wean us; they will refine us; they will blow us to His breast, as a strong wind might sweep a man into some refuge from itself.

2. *The determining factor is our attitude toward the disciplines of life.* But the sorrow that is meant to bring us nearer to Him may be in vain. The same circumstances may produce opposite effects. Take care that you do not waste your sorrows; that you do not let the precious gifts of disappointment, pain, loss, loneliness, ill-health, or similar afflictions that come in your daily life, mar you instead of mending you.

CONCLUSION

Let us try to school ourselves into the habitual and operative conviction that life is discipline. Let us yield ourselves to the loving will of the unerring Father. Let us beware of getting no good from what is charged to the brim with good. Let us see to it that out of the many fleeting circumstances of life we gather and keep the eternal fruit of being partakers of His holiness.

31

Marcus, My Son

So doth Marcus, my son. — I Peter 5:13*

MARK was the son of Mary, a woman of some wealth and position. He was a relative, probably a cousin, of Barnabas and possibly like him, a native of Cyprus. The designation of him by Peter as "my son" naturally implies that the apostle had been the instrument of his conversion.

I. THE WORKING OF CHRISTIAN SYMPATHY.

A. The Change of Name of a Disciple of Christ.

1. *The fact of a change in name.* "John, whose surname was Mark" bore a double name — one Jewish, "John," and one Gentile, "Marcus." As time goes on we do not hear anything more about "John" nor about "John Mark," which are the two forms of his name when he is first introduced to us in the Acts of the Apostles, but he finally appears to have cast aside his Hebrew and to have been only known by his Roman name.

2. *The appropriateness of the change in name in relation to his ministry.* The change of appellation coincides with the fact that so many of the allusions which we have to him represent him as sending messages of Christian greetings to his Gentile brethren. And it further coincides with the fact that his gospel is obviously intended for the use of Gentile Christians.

B. The Significance of the Change in Name.

1. *It intimates a great truth.* This change of name. may be taken as reminding us of a very important truth, that if we

---

* From *Christ's Musts.*

wish to help people, the first condition is that we go down and stand on their level and make ourselves one with them, as far as we can.

2. *The importance of the truth intimated.* Not only the duty of widening our sympathies, but one of the supreme conditions of being of use to anybody is set forth in the comparatively trifling incident, that this man, a Jew to his fingertips, for the sake of efficiency in his work and of getting close by the side of the people whom he wanted to influence, flung away deliberately that which parted him from them.

II. THE POSSIBILITY OF OVERCOMING EARLY FAULTS.

A. The Probable Reason of Mark's Failure.

1. *It might have been the lack of courage to do difficult things.* He was willing to go where he knew the ground and where there were people that would make things easy for him; but when Paul went further afield Mark's courage ebbed out at his finger ends and he slunk back to the comfort of his mother's house in Jerusalem.

2. *The Apostle Paul's view of Mark's failure.* The writer of the Acts puts Paul's view of the case strongly by the arrangement of clauses in the sentence in which he tells us that the Apostle "thought not good to take him with them who withdrew from them from Pamphylia and went not with them to the work" (15:38).

B. The Cure of Mark's Failure.

1. *The evidence of the cure.* The man that was afraid of dangers and difficulties and hypothetical risks became brave enough to stand by the apostle when he was a prisoner. He won his way into the Apostle's confidence and made himself needful for him by his services and his sweetness that the prisoner bids Timothy bring him with himself.

2. *The encouragement of the cure to present day believers.* Translate that from the particular into the general and it

comes to this. Let no man set limits to the possibilities of
his own restoration and of his curing faults which are not
deeply rooted within himself. Hope and effort should be
boundless.

III. THE GREATNESS OF LITTLE SERVICE.

A. The Nature of Mark's Work.

1. *It was to attend to Paul's comfort.* He had to be Paul's man
   of all work; looking after material things, the commissariat,
   the thousand and one trifles that someone had to see to if
   the Apostle's great work was to get done.

2. *It was his life's work.* And he did it all his life long. It was
   enough for him to do thoroughly the entirely "secular"
   work, as some people would think of it, which it was in his
   power to do.

B. The Necessary Requirement to Render Such Service.

1. *Self-suppression.* It would have been so natural for Mark
   to have said, "Paul sends Timothy to be bishop in Crete;
   and Titus to look after other churches; Epaphroditus is an
   official here; and Apollos is a great preacher there. I think
   I'll 'strike' and try and get more conspicuous work." But
   this "minister," a private attendant and valet of the Apostle
   was glad to do that work all his days.

2. *Recognition of the fact that all kinds of work contributing
   to one end are one sort of work.* It was a recognition that
   all sorts of work which contribute to one end are one sort
   of work; and that at bottom the man who carried Paul's
   books and parchments and saw that he was not left without
   clothes was just as much helping on the cause of Christ as
   the Apostle when he preached.

IV. THE ENLARGED SPHERE THAT FOLLOWS
FAITHFULNESS IN SMALL MATTERS.

A. Mark's Enlarged Ministry. The man who began with
being a servant of Paul and of Barnabas ends by being the
evangelist and it is to him under Peter's direction, that we

owe what is possibly the oldest and, at all events, in some aspects, an entirely unique narrative of our Lord's life, "He that is faithful in that which is least is faithful also in much" (Luke 16:10).

B. **The Law That Faithfulness in Little Things Brings Greater Responsibilities.** In God's providence the tools do come to the hand that can wield them and the best reward that we can get for doing well our little work is to have larger work to do. And the law will be exemplified most blessedly when Christ shall say, "Well done! good and faithful servant. Thou has been faithful over a few things, I will make thee ruler over many things" (Matthew 25:21).

CONCLUSION

So this far-away figure of the minister-evangelist salutes us too and bids us be of good cheer, notwithstanding all faults and failures, because it is possible for us, as he has proved, to recover ourselves after them all.

32

The Master and His Slaves

Denying the Lord that bought them.
— II Peter 2:1*

THE apostles glory in calling themselves "slaves of Jesus Christ." That title of honor heads many epistles. In this text we have the same figure expressed with Peter's own energy and carried out in detail. The word in our text for "Lord" is an unusual one, selected to put the idea in the roughest, most absolute form. It is the root of our word "despot" and conveys the notion of unlimited authority.

I. CHRIST'S ABSOLUTE OWNERSHIP.

A. The Sphere of Christ's Lordship.

1. *The realm of nature.* His lips spake and it was done when He was here on earth — rebuking disease, and it fled; the wild storm, and there was a great calm; demons, and they came out; death itself, and its dull, cold ear heard and Lazarus came forth.

2. *The realm of mankind.* His rule in the region of man's spirit is as absolute and authoritative and there too "His word is with power."

B. The Prerogative of Christ's Lordship.

1. *The Master dispenses to His slaves their tasks.* The owner of the slave could set him to any work he thought fit. So our Owner gives all His slaves their several tasks. As in some despotic eastern monarchies the sultan's mere pleasure makes one slave his vizier and another his slipper-bearer, our King chooses one man to a post of honor and

---

* From *The Secret of Power.*

another to a lowly place; none has a right to question the allocation of work.

2. *The Master has first claim on His slave's possessions.* Whose are our possessions? If we have no property in ourselves, still less can we have property in our property. These things were His before and are His still. The first claim on them is our Master's, not ours.

C. The Slave's Response to Christ's Lordship.

1. *Recognition of trusteeship.* If we rightly understand our position we shall feel that we are trustees, not possessors. When, like prodigal sons, we "waste our substance" we are unfaithful stewards, also, "wasting our Lord's goods."

2. Submission to the Master. Such absolute submission of will and recognition of Christ's absolute authority over us, our destiny, work, and possessions is ennobling and blessed. So to bow before a man would be degrading were it possible, but so to bow before Him is our highest honor and liberates us from all other submission.

II. THE PURCHASE ON WHICH OUR OWNERSHIP IS FOUNDED.

A. The Expression of the Purchase. This Master has acquired men by right of purchase. That abomination of the auction-block may suggest the better "merchandise of the souls of men" which Christ has made when He bought us with His own blood as our ransom. That purchase is represented in two forms of expression. Sometimes we read that He has bought us with His "blood"; sometimes that He has given "Himself" for us.

1. *He bought us with His blood.*

2. *He gave Himself for us.*

B. The Reference of the Statements. Both expressions point to the same great fact — His death as the price at which He has acquired us as His own.

C. The Implications of the Text.

1. *Christ's lordship over men is based on His sacrifice for men.*
   That is a very beautiful and profound thought that Christ's
   lordship over men is built upon His mighty and supreme
   sacrifice for men. Nothing short of His utter giving up of
   Himself for them gives Him the right of absolute authority
   over them; or, as Paul puts it, "He gave Himself for us"
   that He might "purchase for Himself a people."

2. *Slaves are purchased from previous slavery.* The figure
   suggests that we are bought from a previous slavery to some
   other master. Free men are not sold into slavery, but slaves
   pass from one master to another and sometimes are bought
   into freedom as well as into bondage. Our Kinsman
   (Christ) bought us back from our bondage to sin and guilt
   and condemnation, from the slavery of our tyrant lusts, from
   the slavery to men's censures and opinions, from the dominion of evil and darkness, and making us His, makes us
   free.

III. THE FUGITIVES OR RUNAWAYS WHO DENY CHRIST'S AUTHORITY.

We do not care to enquire here what special type of heretics
the apostle had in view nor to apply them to modern parallels
which we may fancy we can find. It is more profitable to notice
how all godlessness and sin may be described as denying the Lord.

A. **All Sin is the Denial of Christ's Authority.** It is in effect
   saying, "We will not have this man to reign over us." It is at
   bottom the uprising of our own self-will against His rule and
   the proud assertion of our own independence. It is as foolish
   as it is ungrateful, as ungrateful as it is foolish.

   1. *It is the uprising of self-will against Christ's rule.*

   2. *It is the proud assertion of our own independence.*

B. **The Manifestations of the Denial.** The denial is made by
   deeds which are done in defiance or neglect of His authority
   and it is done too by words and opinions.

1. *It is shown by deeds.*

2. *It is shown by words.*

CONCLUSION

Let us beware lest the fate of many a runaway slave be ours and we be lost in trackless bogs and perish miserably. Casting off His yoke is sure to end in ruin. Rather, drawn by the cords of love and owning the blessed bonds in which willing souls are held by the love of Christ, let us take Him for our Lord, who has given Himself for our ransom and answer the pleading of His cross with our glad surrender.

33

For the Sake of the Name

For His name's sake. — III John 7*

THE Revised Version gives the true force of these words by omitting the "His" and reading merely "for the sake of the Name." The word rendered "for the sake of" does not merely mean — though it does mean that — "on account of" or "by reason of," but "on behalf of," as if, in some wonderful sense that mighty and exalted Name was furthered, advantaged, or benefited by even man's poor services.

I. THE PREEMINENCE IMPLIED IN "THE NAME."

A. The Meaning of "the Name."

1. *"The Name" stands for the person and work of Christ.* "The Name" means the whole Christ as we know Him or as we may know Him from the Book, in His messiahship, deity, life, words, sacrifice, resurrection, ascension, and present life and reigning work for us at the right hand of God.

2. *"The Name" indicates the supremacy of Christ in His person and work.* It is but a picturesque and condensed way of saying that Jesus Christ, in the depth of His nature and the width of His work, stands alone and is the single, because the all-sufficient object of love and trust and obedience.

B. The Demands of "the Name." The uniqueness and solitariness of "the Name" demands an equal and corresponding exclusiveness of devotion and trust.

---

* From *The God of the Amen.*

1. *The demand of implicit trust.* There is one Christ and there is none other but He. Therefore all the current of my being is to set to Him and on Him alone am I to repose my undivided weight, casting all my cares and putting all my trust only on Him.

2. *The demand of implicit devotion.* Love none other except Him; for His heart is wide enough and deep enough for all mankind. Obey none other, for only His voice has the right to command. And lifting up our eyes, let us see "No man any more save Jesus only." That Name stands alone.

C. The Intimation of "the Name."

1. *It implies the deity of Christ.* The preeminent and exclusive mention of the Name carries with it, in fair inference, the declaration of His Divine nature. It seems impossible that a man saturated as this Apostle was with Old Testament teaching and familiar as he was as to the sanctity of "the Name of the Lord," should have used such language as this of my text unless he had felt, as he has told us himself, that "the Word was God."

2. *It implies the common acknowledgement of the deity of Christ by the Apostolic Church.* The very incidental character of the allusion gives it the more force as a witness to the common-placeness which the thought of the deity of Jesus Christ had assumed to the consciousness of the Christian Church.

II. THE POWER OF THE NAME TO SWAY THE LIFE.

A. There is Guidance.

1. *Wherein it lies.* In Him, in the whole fulness of His being, in the wonders of the story of His character and historical manifestation, there lies all guidance for men.

2. *What Christ is to us.* He is the pattern of our conduct. He is the Companion for us in our sorrow. He is the Quickener but shall have the light of life.
of the Name" the motto of his life will not walk in darkness, for us in all of our tasks. Whosoever makes "for the sake

B. There is Power.

1. *It is the secret of the transformation of lives.* There is
nothing else that will go so deep down into the heart and
unseal the fountains of power and obedience as that Name.
There is nothing else that will so strike the shackles off the
prisoned will and fan back to their caves the wild beasts that
tyrannize within and put the chain round their necks as the
Name of Jesus Christ.

2. *It flows from the Cross of Christ.* Where in the life and work
of Jesus Christ is the dominant summit from which the
streams run down? The Cross! The love that died for us is
the thing that draws out answering love. And answering
love is the power that transmutes my whole nature into the
humble aspiration to be like Him and to render back myself
unto Him for His gift.

III. THE SERVICE THAT WE CAN RENDER TO THE NAME.

A. The Evidence That Believers Can Give Beneficial Service to the Lord.

1. *The testimony of the context.* There were some Christian
people who had gone on a missionary tour and penniless and
homeless they had come to a city and had been taken in and
kindly entertained by a Christian brother. And says John,
these humble men went out "on behalf of the Name." Jesus
Christ the bearer of the Name, was in some sense helped and
benefited by the work of these lowly and unknown brethren.

2. *The testimony of additional Scriptures.* Acts 5:41; 9:16;
15:26; 21:13; Romans 1:5. If we put all these together
they just come to this, that He has appointed that His
Name should be furthered by the sufferings, the service, the
life, and the death of His followers.

B. The Manner in Which Service Can be Rendered to the Lord.

1. *By word of mouth.* "He was extolled with my tongue," says
the Psalmist in a rapture of wonder that any words of his

could extol God's Name. So to you Christians is committed
the charge of magnifying the Name of Jesus Christ.

2. *By life.* We can "adorn the doctrine" and make men think
more highly of our Lord by our example of faithfulness and
obedience. If from us sounded out the Name and over all
that we did it was written blazing, conspicuous, the world
would look and listen and men would believe that there was
something in the Gospel.

CONCLUSION

If you are a professing Christian either Christ is glorified or
put to shame in you, His saint; and either it is true of you that
you do all things in the Name of the Lord Jesus and so glorify His
Name or that through you the Name of Christ is "blasphemed
among the nations." Choose which of the two it shall be.

34

How to Keep in the Love of God

> *But ye, beloved, building up yourselves on your most holy faith, praying in the Holy Ghost, keep yourselves in the love of God, looking for the mercy of our Lord Jesus Christ unto eternal life.* — Jude 20, 21*

THE main subject of this letter is the warning against certain teachers whose errors of belief and vice of conduct seem to have been equally great. After the denunciation of these the writer turns, as with a sudden movement of revulsion, from the false teachers to exhort his readers to conduct contrary to theirs, and sets forth in these words the true way by which individuals and churches can guard themselves against abounding errors.

I. THE CENTRAL INJUNCTION: "Keep yourselves in the love of God."

A. What is Meant by the Love of God? Now "the love of God" here obviously means not ours to Him, but His to us, and the commandment is parallel to and may be a reminiscence of our Lord's great word: "As the Father hath loved Me, so have I loved you. Continue ye in My love" (John 15:9).

1. *Negatively stated: it is not our love to God.*

2. *Positively stated: it is God's love to us.*

B. Can a Man Get Out of the Love of God?

1. *God's love always extends to all men.* No doubt "His tender mercies are over all His works" (Psalm 145:9). No doubt His love holds in a grasp which never can be loosened every creature that He has made.

---

*From *The Unchanging Christ.*

2. *The blessings and consciousness of God's love may be lost.*
All the best and noblest manifestations of that love and the
sweetest, most select aspects of that love cannot come to
men irrespective of their moral character and their relation
to Him. It is possible for Christian people to lose the consciousness of being surrounded and kept within that warm
and sunny circle where God's love falls.

C. Can a Man Always Keep in the Love of God?

1. *The ideal set forth in the text.* The ideal set forth here is
that of unbroken continuity in the flow of that Divine love
which falls in its gentlest and mightiest beams only upon
the heart that aspires towards Him, and also a continual
consciousness on my part that I am within the reach of its
rays and that it is well with me because I am.

2. *The experience of many Christians.* Instead of one unbroken line of light, what do we find? A dot of light and
then a stretch of blackness; and then another little sparkle,
scarcely visible, and short lived, followed by another dreary
tract of murky midnight.

3. *The secret of all blessedness.* The secret of all blessedness
is to live in the love of God. Our sorrows and difficulties
and trials will change their aspect if we walk in the peaceful
enjoyment and conscious possession of His Divine heart.
That is the true anesthetic.

II. THE SUBSIDIARY EXHORTATIONS WHICH POINT OUT THE MEANS OF OBEYING THE CENTRAL COMMAND.

A. A Continual Building Up of a Noble Character on the Foundation of Faith.

1. *Faith is only the basis of spiritual progress.* The foundation
of all that is good and noble in a character is the going out
of self to trust in God manifest in Christ. That is the real
basis of everything that is great and lofty. But the faith
which is thus the foundation of all excellence is only the
foundation.

2. *Continuous effort is the condition of spiritual progress.* Then remember, too, that this building of a noble and god-like and God-pleasing character can be erected on the foundation of faith only by constant effort. Continuous effort is the condition of progress.

3. *The importance of continual spiritual progress.* They, and only they, have a right to say, "I believe in God the Father and in Jesus Christ His Son," in whom their faith is daily producing growth in the grace as well as in the knowledge which have Him for their object.

B. Holy Spirit Directed Prayer.

1. *The necessity of prayer.* Who that has ever honestly tried to cure himself of a fault or to make his own some unfamiliar virtue opposed to his natural temperament, but has found that the cry "O God! help me" has come instinctively to his lips.

2. *The nature of prayer.* The prayer which helps us to keep in the love of God is not the petulant and passionate utterance of our own wishes, but is the yielding of our desires to the impulses divinely breathed upon us.

3. *The effectiveness of prayer.* My prayer breaks the bond of many a temptation that holds me. My prayer is the test for many a masked evil that seeks to seduce me. My prayer will be like a drop of poison on a scorpion — it will kill the sin on the instant.

III. THE EXPECTATION ATTENDANT ON THE OBEDIENCE TO THE CENTRAL COMMANDMENT: Looking for the mercy of the Lord Jesus Christ unto eternal life.

A. The Call for Mercy. The best of us, looking back over our past, will most deeply feel that it is all so poor and stained that all we have to trust to is the forgiving mercy of our Lord Jesus Christ.

B. The Anticipation for Mercy. That mercy will be anticipated for all the future in proportion as we keep ourselves for the present in the love of God. The more we feel in our hearts the experience that God loves us, the more sure shall we be that He will love us ever.

C. **The Ground for Hope in Christ's Future Mercy.** The consciousness of His present love is the surest ground for the hope in Christ's future mercy.

D. **The Blessings of Mercy.** That mercy will scatter its pardoning gifts all along the path of life and will not reach its highest issue nor be satisfied in its relation to us until it has brought us into the full and perfect enjoyment of that super-eminent degree of eternal life which lies beyond the grave.

CONCLUSION

If you and I keep ourselves in the love of God by effort founded upon faith and prospered by prayer, we may then look quietly forward to that solemn future, knowing our sins indeed, but sure of the love of God and therefore sure of eternal life.

A New Name

> *To him that overcometh will I give . . . a
> new name . . . which no man knoweth
> saving he that receiveth it.*
>
> — Revelation 2:17*

THE series of sevenfold promises attached to these letters to the Asiatic churches presents us with a sevenfold aspect of future blessedness. In the present case the little community at Pergamos was praised because it held fast Christ's name and so there is promised to it a new name as its very own.

I. THE LARGE HOPES WHICH GATHER ROUND THIS PROMISE OF A NEW NAME.

A. The "New Name" Means a New Vision. We know not how much the flesh, which is the organ of perception for things sensible, is an obscurity, blind, and impenetrable barrier between us and the loftier order of things unseen. But this we know, that when the stained glass of life is shattered, the white light of eternity will pour in. "Now we see through a glass darkly: then, face to face" (I Corinthians 13:12).

B. The "New Name" Means New Activities. We know not how far these fleshly organs, which are the condition of our working upon the outward universe with which they bring us into connection, limit and hem the operations of the spirit. But this we know, that when that which is sown in weakness is raised in power (I Corinthians 15:43), we shall then possess an instrument adequate to all that we can ask it to perform; a perfect tool for a perfected spirit.

---

*From *The Unchanging Christ.*

148

C. **The "New Name" Means New Purity.** There are two words very characteristic of this book of the Apocalypse. One of them is that word of my text, "new." The other is "white," not the cold, pallid white that may mean death, but the flashing white, as of sunshine upon snow, the radiant white of purity smitten by Deity and so blazing up into lustre that dazzles. The one element in the newness of the "new name" is spotless purity and supernal radiance.

D. **The "New Name" Means New Joys.** Here and now we know joy and sorrow as a double star, one bright and the other dark, which revolve around one center and with terrible swiftness take each others places. But there, "Thou makest them drink of the river of thy pleasures" (Psalm 36:8). A joy after the pattern of His joy, that was full and abode — an undisturbed and changing blessedness.

II. THE CONNECTION BETWEEN CHRIST'S NEW NAME AND OURS.

A. **The Promise That Christ's New Name Will Be Written Upon the Overcomer.** In Revelation 4:12 we read, "Him that overcometh will I make a pillar in the Temple of My God, and I will write upon him . . . My new name." The new name of Jesus in a revelation of His character; a new manifestation of Himself to the eyes of those that loved Him when they saw Him amidst the darkness and mists of earth. It implies no antiquating of the old name. Nothing will make the Cross of Christ less the center of the revelation of God than it is today.

B. **The Significance of Christ's New Name Inscribed Upon the Overcomer.** It is not merely the manifestation of the revealed character of Jesus in new beauty, but it is the manifestation of His ownership of His servants by transformation into His likeness, which transformation is the consequence of their new vision of Him. It is but saying in other words, "The new revelation of My character, which he shall receive, will be stamped upon his character and he shall become like Myself."

III. THE BLESSED SECRET OF THIS NEW NAME.

A. It is Known Only to the Receiver. "No man knoweth it saving he that receiveth it." Of course not. There is only one way to know the highest things in human experience and that is by possessing them. That is eminently true about religion and it is most of all true about that perfect future state.

B. It is A Mystery to All But the Receiver. That same blessed mystery lies round about the name of each individual possessor, to all but himself. Each eye shall see its own rainbow and each will possess in happy certitude of individual possession a honeyed depth of sweet experience, which will remain unrevealed, the basis of the being, the deep function of the blessedness. But it will be a mystery of no painful darkness, nor making any barrier between ourselves and the saints whom we love.

C. It Guarantees Variety in the Possession of the One Name. All the surrounding diamonds that are set about the central blaze shall catch the light on their facets, and from one it will come golden, and from another red, and another flashing and pure white. Each glorified spirit shall reveal Christ and yet the one Christ shall be manifested in infinite variety of forms and the total summing up of the many reflections will be the image of the whole Lord.

IV. THE GIVING OF THE NEW NAME TO THE VICTORS.

A. The Condition Laid Down: "To him that overcometh." This renovation of the being, and efflorescence into new knowledges, activities, perfections, and joy is only possible on condition of the earthly life of obedience and service and conquest. It is no arbitrary bestowment of a title. The conqueror gets the name that embodies his victories, and without conquering a man cannot receive it.

B. The Cause Laid Down: "Will I give." But while the conquering life here is the condition of the gift, it is none the less a gift. It is not a case of evolution but of bestowal by

God's free love in Christ. The power by which we conquer is
His gift and when He crowns it, it is His own grace in it which
He crowns.

CONCLUSION

So my friends, here is the all important truth for us all. "This
is the victory that overcometh the world, even our faith (I John
5:4); and that faith is victorious in idea and germ as soon as it
begins to abide in a man's heart. We shall either conquer by
Christ's strength and so receive His Divine name or else be beaten
by the world and the flesh and the devil and so bear the image of
our conquerors.